Burnt
Toast

Burnt Toast

AND OTHER PHILOSOPHIES OF LIFE

TERI HATCHER

HYPERION

NEW YORK

Visit Teri's website . . . www.myburnttoast.com

Illustrations by Colleen Ross

Library of Congress Cataloging-in-Publication Data
Hatcher, Teri.
    Burnt toast: and other philosophies of life / Teri Hatcher —1st. ed.
      p. cm.
    ISBN 1-4013-0262-9
    1. Hatcher, Teri. 2. Television actors and actresses—United States—
Biography. 3. Conduct of life. I. Title.
PN2287.H32A3 2006
791.4502'8092—dc22
[B]   2005055016

Hyperion books are available for special promotions and premiums. For details contact Michael
Rentas, Assistant Director, Inventory Operations, Hyperion, 77 West 66th Street, 12th floor,
New York, New York 10023, or call 212-456-0133.

Design by Nicola Ferguson

FIRST EDITION

10 9 8 7 6 5 4 3 2 1

To Emerson, whose birth was the sole source of my personal evolution over the last seven years. Thank you for giving my life meaning. I will try not to eat as much burnt toast as my mom did—and maybe you won't eat any ever.

And to my mother, for doing her best and for giving me material to write a book.

Contents

Burnt
Toast

Introduction
Burnt Toast

Toast. Think about it for a moment. It probably has the simplest recipe in the world: one ingredient, one instruction. Still, you know when you're trying to make it and you just can't get it right? It's too light or too soft, then ... totally burnt. Charred in a matter of seconds—now it's more like a brick than a piece of toast. So what do you do? Are you the kind of person who tries to scrape off the black? Or do you smother it with jam to hide the taste? Do you throw it away, or do you just eat it? If you shrug and eat the toast, is it because you're willing to settle for less? Maybe you don't want to be wasteful, but if you go ahead and eat that blackened square of bread, then what you're really saying—to yourself and to the world—is that the piece of bread is worth more than your own satisfaction.

Up 'til now, I ate the burnt toast. I learned that from my mother—metaphorically if not literally. I can't actually remember if she even likes toast or how she eats it. But what I know for sure is that although she was a loving and devoted wife and mother, she always took care of everyone and everything else before herself. This habitual self-sacrifice was well intended, but ultimately it's a mixed message for a child. It taught me that in order for me to succeed, someone else had to suffer. I learned to accept whatever was in front of me without complaint because I didn't think I deserved good things.

I can toast bread just fine. I don't know about you, but my toaster only has one button. It's a no-brainer. And still, I've been eating that metaphoric burnt toast all my life, and I think other people do too. Then I hit forty. Jules Renard said, "We don't understand life any better at forty than at twenty, but we know it and admit it." Admitting that there were things I still needed to figure out made me see this new decade as a chance to reconsider some of my behaviors. Did I really want to spend another ten years this way? The easy answer: no. The harder realization was that in order to change, I needed to stop eating the burnt toast. I had to be done anticipating failure. I had to be done feeling like I didn't deserve good things, tasty things. And I was. I decided I was too old to continue this way. I didn't want to do it anymore, and I don't want other people to do it either. There is a way for us to value ourselves without taking away from anyone else. We should settle for nothing less than being good to ourselves and others. But it's hard to break old habits. You can make a new piece of toast in a couple minutes, but happiness takes work. That's why I wrote this book. It's my wacky, serious, skittish, heartfelt attempt to share my jagged route to happiness with other people like me.

Toast is small and simple, and maybe eating a lousy piece of it doesn't seem like the worst thing in the world. Agreed. I can think of far worse things. But this isn't a book about surviving worst-case scenarios. It's about weathering the small challenges that we encounter every day. This scar that I have on my left shin might give you an idea of what I'm talking about. I got it when I was at the beach with my daughter, Emerson Rose. It was the first morning of our trip, and Emerson and I spent it playing in the sand and walking along the beach. In front of our hotel, about fifteen feet off the shore in a calm area of the ocean, there was a floating trampoline. Pretty cool, huh? I'd never seen that before. It looked like it was *intended* to be fun, but was it something I really wanted to do? Not so much. I didn't want to be bouncing around in front of the whole beach in my less-than-supportive bikini. Nor did I want to plunge into the deep, dark ocean to swim out to the trampoline. Wading was just fine with me. Before I was a mother, I wouldn't have gone near something like that. But I am a mother now, and I could see that Emerson was afraid, but curious. As a single mom I find myself in this situation a lot—there's some adventure that doesn't appeal to me, but there's no one I can turn to and say, "Your turn, honey. Take Emerson out onto the trampoline." Same thing when there's a spider on the wall above the bed. That eight-legged intruder's got to go, and it's all me.

We swam out to the trampoline and bounced around for a while. Then Emerson wanted to jump off, but she was scared. I said, "Oh sure, let's do it. It'll be really fun. I'll go first." Now you and I both know that I did *not* want to jump off that trampoline. I was scared. But I don't want to teach that to her. I don't want to project my overblown imaginative worries onto her wide-eyed innocent hope. Now the thing about this floating trampoline is that it wasn't very bouncy, and what little bounce it had was weird and off-kilter, so you couldn't really plan your trajectory. But my daughter was waiting and watching, so what could I do? I flew off the trampoline into—a huge belly flop. A belly flop looks funny. It even sounds funny. But I'm here to say: It's. Not. Funny. My stomach, my arms, my legs—all my skin burned. I was instantly red and tender all over, but I didn't want Emerson to see that I was in serious pain. That wasn't the lesson I wanted to teach. I knew she could do it and I knew that she, unlike her aging mom, would be fine. So I popped my head out of the water and said, "That was so fun! Give it a try." She jumped straight off, loved it, of course, and did it again and again. When we got back to the beach, I saw that I had a long cut on my leg from the water (who knew that could happen?). Emerson noticed the blood, and I shrugged it off with some stupid excuse. I was in agony, but I didn't want to cry in front of Emerson. Instead, I got a rum-infused coconut beverage from the guy walking down the beach and subtly iced my wound.

Now I look at the scar on my leg and wonder if I did the right thing. Should I have let Emerson know that I was hurt? Should I have called over a (preferably cute) lifeguard for some first aid? Why didn't I do that? Why did I hide the truth about what was going on with me? Did I do it for her or for me? Was I trying to be cool or tough? There's an emotional experience embedded in that scar. There's a lesson locked in it. I'm done making silent self-sacrifices. I'm done hiding the truth. Here it is. Have at it.

I hope you'll discover as you read this book that vulnerability plays a key role in my life. It's hard for me—I have trouble admitting that I need other people. I've always tried to be honest about my fears and insecurities and self-doubt. When I was doing the photo shoot for the cover of this book, I spent the first hour thinking, *This is ridiculous. I haven't even written the book yet.* (I guess this is how they do things in the world of publishing—they need the jacket before the book's done.) So I was up there posing and thinking, *Maybe there is no book. Maybe I have nothing to say. Maybe I'm just an idiot. Who do I think I am?* Then I started talking to the photographer and the makeup guy and the wardrobe guy and the photo assistants. We were laughing and feeling good, and suddenly someone revealed that, like me, he'd had no sex on his honeymoon. We both had felt embarrassed and inadequate, like we were the only people in the history of time who couldn't get it together to have sex on a honeymoon. And I said, "See, we really are all the same!" Maybe this is too much information for an introduction— I'm already telling you about my sex life (or sad lack thereof) and I'm only on page 4. (It was the publisher's mandate—write whatever you want so long as you mention sex before Chapter 2.) But that's what this book is about—how when we feel fragile and vulnerable and hopeful and human, we're not alone. And if I can have these feelings and work through them then you can too. My hope for this book is that you'll read it in the bathtub. Maybe with a glass of wine. And that you'll laugh a little and feel a little inspired.

Just because I'm up front about this stuff doesn't mean I've figured it all out. Not even close. Even if I do have some good ideas about how to help you live a happier life, I'm not sure I always practice them, and I certainly don't practice them every day. It's too hard. Some days I'm like Alice, trapped deep down in that rabbit hole. And instead of trying to find my way out, I just hide away, watch B movies until I can't keep my eyes open, and then sleep for a really long time. But I rarely have time for that self-indulgence, so I put on my mom clothes or my "Teri Hatcher" costume, as I like to call it, and pretend everything's fine.

In my scrapbook from 1999 there's a fortune-cookie fortune that says, "Your luck has been completely changed today." But you don't change in a day. Just because you're getting older or more successful doesn't mean you automatically grow as a human being. You learn things when life presents you with an opportunity and you're ready to receive it. When *Desperate Housewives* came along, I was, like many an aging female actress in Hollywood, a big has-been. I've made no secret of that. I never expected to get a second chance, though I must have saved that fortune in hope that everything actually could change overnight. When it did, when *Desperate Housewives* became a hit, I suddenly had the job and security and affirmation that I'd given up on long before.

Over time, when they don't come true, you lose sight of your dreams. Years go by and you look back and wonder how you got so far without starting a band, making a sculpture, doing the things that you wanted to do but couldn't because now you have a family or kids or a mortgage. For whatever reason, it didn't ever happen. So when my dream actually became reality, my response wasn't "better late than never." I'd just turned forty, was a divorced mom of a young daughter, and I didn't want to simply ride my wave of success. I wanted to live it—not as the twenty-year-old who desired it, but as the forty-year-old who worked hard for it but thought her opportunity had passed. It woke me up to the realization that though life is unpredictable, things can change for the better, dreams we thought were long past can still come true, and that we increase our chances of that happening by believing that we are deserving—of golden-brown buttered toast, and success and happiness. Mmm. I'm getting hungry.

I wrote most of this book sitting on the floor in my living room. I like the floor. There's no place to fall. The first time I sat down with a little blank book, a pen, and the mandate from my editor to start writing down my thoughts and feelings, I stared at the page. Before I could hook any of the ideas that worm their way in and out of my tired brain, I just sat there in awe. *Wow. I have an editor.* I wrote that down. *And crappy penmanship.* I wrote that down too. *Yeah, I'm finally old enough, used enough, hailed enough to put some of it on paper.* That got me started. I kept going until the first page was almost full and I was on to the next, but my hand was starting to hurt. I'd finally seen, touched, and tasted enough; I'd loved, struggled, and learned enough to have a tale to tell, and my hand was having an arthritic attack. Leave it to me to figure out how to stand in my own way. Time after time as I shuffled through scrawled notes and fragmented thoughts, I was paralyzed by my lack of confidence. This wasn't an unfamiliar state of affairs. No matter what the challenge before me—an audition, a photo shoot, writing a book, or a relationship—for all my past accomplishments, I torture myself on the way, always wondering, *Why would they pick me? Why am I good enough to do this? He'll never like me as much as I like him. Who the hell do I think I am—I'm not that special.* This book itself was a journey for me. Writing it forced me to face my self-doubt and fears—the same kind of struggles that this book contemplates. I kept thinking, *I need to read this book.* In fact,

I'll probably be the first one to buy a copy because then a) I'll know that at least one copy sold and b) I really will be able to remind myself of the lessons I've learned every once in a while.

The lessons here are about how to forgive, love, enjoy, and explore yourself as a woman. I've finally gotten to a place where I'm easier on myself. I'm comfortable and happy being a mother. Being in my body. Feeling sensual as a forty-year-old woman. Most of the time. I sure hope you're one of the people who managed to have sex at some point during your honeymoon. Good for you! But if you've ever felt like a spicy gumbo of fear and confidence, despair and hope, desire and satisfaction, mother and child, pretty and ugly, strong and weak, then read on. The journey's a whole lot easier if we take it together.

Chickening Out

Imagine this. It's a sunny Sunday and you're meeting some friends for a picnic at a lovely spot that's mere minutes from your home. (Hey, it's a fantasy—we might as well make it convenient.) You're in a great mood, and you even brought a yummy gourmet lunch that someone else prepared. (Again: fantasy.) When you arrive at your idyllic, balmy destination, it turns out there's a lake, with an outcropping of rock jutting out over it to form a natural high-dive. It's high enough to be scary, but low enough to be safe. There are screams of joy as an endless line of people jump off. Okay, now here's where I want you to drop the fantasy and consider the situation as if it were real. The question is: Are you the kind of person who climbs right up, takes in the view for a fraction of a second, then plunges off the edge without a second thought? Or do you stand there, trying to get your guts up to jump, and after a few minutes decide it's too scary and climb back down, admitting defeat? Are you the daredevil, or the wimp? The good news (I hope) is that I'm not here to talk about how brave the first person is, and how the second person is a pluckless chicken who should learn to face the world with guts and determination. No, the way I see it is—if you're either of these people, you're lucky. You know what makes you happy, you know your limits, and that's that. But some of us are stuck in the middle, making life a whole lot more complicated than that. I'm the one who found myself standing frozen at the top of a twenty-five-foot-high rock platform looking down at a placid Sedona lake. I'm the one who stood there, not for ten minutes. Not for half an hour. I stood there for *over an hour* trying to convince myself to jump. *Torturing* myself over this pointless, supposedly fun activity. Half terrified. Half hating my own terror. Half wanting to be the kind of person who jumped. Half wanting to climb down and eat some potato salad. That's right. Four halves. That's what I'm talking about: a schizophrenic war with myself.

After a good hour and fifteen minutes, I finally jumped off that stupid rock. By then I was so tired of arguing with myself that I was ready to kill myself anyway, so what harm could it possibly do? I did it. I jumped. When I surfaced, there was some biker guy by the edge of the lake clapping for me. He said, "That's the longest I've seen anyone stand up there looking and *still jump*." That's me. I may be scared and conflicted about something, but I go through with it. And for what? Was it fun? Are you kidding me? It was completely anticlimactic. It's just like sex—too much deliberation kills the mood. It wasn't even close to fun. All I gained from my jump was the right to tell myself that I hadn't given up. I'd passed another self-imposed test. Yay me.

You know what they say—you can tell a lot about a person by how they jump off a cliff. Okay, maybe they don't say that. But it's not just an isolated afraid-of-heights type of thing. Not for me, anyway. It's part of my everyday life—that top-of-a-cliff fear, hyper-analysis, internal conflict. That circular contemplation of how I feel, who I am, and who I want to be that keeps me paralyzed on cliff tops for ridiculously long periods of time. I've always doubted my abilities and had trouble acknowledging my own success. Take a bet I once made regarding a limousine. If you think I stood on that cliff for a long time . . . let me tell you, the limo thing went on for years.

It started when I first moved to Los Angeles. I was living in North Hollywood. My next-door neighbor, I'll call him Ned*, didn't have a refrigerator and one day he asked to borrow ice and we became friends. (What kind of girl actually believes a guy who knocks on her door to borrow ice? Me, that's who. Nineteen years old, fresh off the Silicon Valley chipwagon, and plopped into a city where the women were faster than the cars.) Anyway, along the way Ned and I made a deal. It was after I got my first part, playing a dancing, singing, lounge act mermaid on *The Love Boat,* and the agreement was that whoever of us became a star first had to rent a limousine. Then we'd spend a whole day driving around in our glamorous stretch limo. Doing what? Doing regular errands: going to McDonald's, picking up the dry cleaning, buying ice (Ned only—he had to keep up the charade). We'd just cruise around doing nothing out of the ordinary, as if renting a limo were just another ho-hum part of our lives. Nothing was further from the truth. I could barely afford the dry cleaning that we would theoretically go to pick up. Growing up, our family car was an orange Chevy Vega with a black stripe down the middle and Neil Sedaka permanently stuck in the eight track. The only limo I'd ever been in was the one my date and his friends rented for my senior prom, and it was white, which (I now know) is absolutely unacceptable in Hollywood. To me, limo equaled private jet equaled swimming pool filled with Dom Perignon—none of which I'd ever seen, ridden in, or dove into. Extravagant beyond what I ever imagined I could experience.

When push came to shove, I wasn't good for the limo bet. When I

---

*I don't want anyone out there to think I'm the kind of friend who reveals personal details, so to protect the innocent who knew me then (when they didn't have to worry about tabloids) and the not-so-innocent who know me now, I've changed names throughout this book.

had my *TV Guide* debut for a short stint on a soap opera, *Capitol*, Ned said, "You made it! You're in *TV Guide*. Looks like you owe me a limo ride." But I shook my head. No way could I accept that I'd been successful at anything. "Not yet. I haven't made it yet." In fact, I kept my waitress job at an Italian joint in the Valley and worked there after filming the soap opera all day. Time passed, and eventually I got my first part in a feature movie, *The Big Picture*. Well, when Ned heard the news, he said, "Okay. This is the big time. You're in a movie, and it even has the word 'big' in the title. Now where's our limo?" But still I resisted. It became an ongoing joke between us—when I got my second and third movies, when I got cast in *Lois & Clark*, I always argued, "I'm a small fish in a big movie!" or found some other reason that it didn't count—why I still hadn't "made it." It may sound like I was an ambitious go-getter, never satisfied, always needing to climb to the next rung. But I was actually just full of doubt. I was too worried that it would all disappear overnight, that the acting police would come pounding on my door at 3 A.M. with documents revealing that my only acting education was a six-week summer program at American Conservatory Theater in San Francisco, demanding my Screen Actors Guild card back and accusing me of fraudulent claims of talent and attempted mugging (the face kind, not the purse-snatching kind). I couldn't revel in my success—even when it came. Sort of like finally jumping off the cliff into that lake in Sedona. By the time I managed to get there, I was long past enjoying it.

Self-doubt runs deep. I've been this way my whole life. It's hard to pinpoint why. It's not like your parents sit down and figure out the best way to screw you up and then embark on an organized execution of the plan. Sometimes I wish that life could be more like golf. I know, I know, if there are two things the world doesn't need any more of it's types of wine openers and analogies about golf, but bear with me. Unless you take the game super-seriously (you know, the type who throws his club at the duck that quacked during his tee shot), which I don't, each shot is a brand-new opportunity, totally disconnected from the shot before and the shot after. Each hole is a new chance to perform and succeed and be a great golfer. Golf is zen like that. But that's not how life works. Small decisions, occasional traumas, incidental inconsistencies—everything adds up in odd, unpredictable, conflicted ways. Each moment is weighed down by its own set of baggage from the past, and we're messy bundles of self-protection and reaction to our uneven, unchoreographed experiences.

In early high school, when I was taking geometry, I remember showing my math-genius dad a problem I'd solved correctly. I probably hoped he'd be proud that I was learning a little bit of his field. He looked at the paper and said, "You know, there are three other ways to solve that problem." I said, "I got it right, didn't I?" I wasn't really interested in alternate solutions. I'd managed to do it the way the teacher had taught us and that was enough. He handed the paper back to me and said, "You're a brick." He didn't mean it in the jolly old English use of "brick," as a dependable chap. Nor was he referring to my abs. He went on, "You should be a sponge, but you're a brick." He meant that I wasn't as open-minded or curious as he wanted me to be. I had shown my dad my correctly done math homework, and he in turn found something wrong with me. Getting the right answer wasn't enough.

He was also the kind of dad who always beat me at chess and ping-pong. I think he just never found the balance of trying to teach me to be good at something, and realizing that since I was a child it was highly unlikely that I'd ever beat him at anything (he's changed as a grandfather). I wonder if he thought he was building my character by continually reminding me that I wasn't good enough to win, or if he thought losing shouldn't matter to me. But it did. As a kid, if you lose enough times you quit trying. You have to be taught the balance between the effort it takes to improve and a realistic view of your capabilities.

My mother, on the other hand, thought everything I did was perfect. She thought constant praise was the way to show love and build self-esteem. But if you're perfect in your mother's eyes, imagine how far you fall when you find out you aren't perfect in the eyes of the world. And no kid is, not even me, though if you look up "goody-goody" in the dictionary, you'll find my name. So I had one parent teaching me to lose and the other teaching false confidence. Parents can fall into traps like this. If yours were anything like mine, they didn't mean to be harmful. I learned to be a loser, to manage failure, to expect that even my best efforts wouldn't fulfill expectations, and that I would never be good enough at anything. Ironically, I became great at having that attitude.

When I was fourteen or fifteen, I auditioned for the San Francisco Ballet. I went with some of the other girls in my dance class. I knew they were all better than I was, and, not surprisingly, I didn't get in. I still have the rejection letter. Why save it, you might wonder. Was it that important to me? Was I that heartbroken? Not exactly. But the scrapbook I made while in high school had a section titled "Failures," and that's where I kept the letter of rejection, along with a few photos of ex-boyfriends. How's that for being a good loser? I kept a record of my losses the way others might carefully preserve their ribbons and medals. Like I wanted to have a physical place to affirm the notion that I was *not* good. (Can you say *therapy*? Don't worry, I got there eventually.)

I may have been a brick instead of a sponge, but I still ended up a math major in college. (Well, junior college. I'd been planning to transfer to Cal Poly, but I never made it. Who wouldn't sideline calculus for a chance to work for Captain Stubing?) Maybe that's why I tend to look at my life as if it's a problem to be solved. I calculate all the possible scenarios—or at least all the bad ones—analyzing, judging, protecting, defending. Like there must be a right answer if only I could find it. But there isn't and I can't. Life isn't two plus two equals four. I wish it were that simple and clear cut.

You only get one life, and it's supposed to be fun, isn't it? Of course we all have to work, but isn't the point of working hard to succeed and to use that success to secure yourself a well-earned, hearty chunk of fun? Having fun is letting go. Letting go of all that analyzing and planning and second-guessing yourself. But it can be really hard to do. In small doses, cautious doubt is healthy—you keep things in perspective and don't set yourself up for disappointment. But I let it get out of control. And sometimes that doubt creeps into other parts of my life— from my friendships to my social life to exercise to work.

It's really easy for me to foresee my own failure. If I'm trying out for a part I tell myself, *They'll want someone younger. Or blonde. Or left-handed*. Basically, they won't want *me*. But I still try as hard as I can. It's all a silent, internal battle that I try not to let have a visible effect unless, or until, something brings it to the surface. Around the same time I was up for a part in *Desperate Housewives*, I was also up for a part in another ABC show—a sitcom. A sitcom can be an easier gig than an hour-long show, at least in terms of the work schedule and hours. So I figured that even though I loved the *Desperate Housewives* script, the sitcom was my top choice since it jibed better with my priorities as a single mom.

I went in to test for the sitcom first, doing a scene in front of some network executives from ABC. I felt comfortable; people laughed; I thought I did great. That night, I waited for the phone to ring and . . . nothing. Nothing that night. Nothing the next day. I was having a nervous breakdown. When I finally heard back, I hadn't gotten the part. Okay, that's happened before—just another memento for the failures page. But what killed me was that word came back that somebody in the room thought I had an attitude. Like I had a chip on my shoulder or thought I was too fancy to audition. Well, that sent me reeling. I couldn't believe it. It was so untrue. It's even hard to share this story with you because I worry some of you will believe I *did* have an attitude—you remember that feeling you had when you were a kid and your parents thought you were lying about something and you weren't, but there was no way you were going to change their minds?

When I was fifteen I was at my boyfriend's house. My mom came to pick me up in our Chevy Vega, and before we drove a block, she pulled over and insisted that I'd been smoking pot. Well, I hadn't and I told her so. Hell, I didn't even know what pot was. (I wasn't kidding about that goody-goody thing.) But she kept insisting she could smell it on my breath. What happened to being innocent until proven guilty? I guess that constitutional right went out the Vega window and was replaced with her lack of confidence that I was an honest person whom she could trust to just answer a question directly. No, somehow I'd become a plotting, manipulative bad seed and it was my mother's obligation to shuck me out. Well, I did prove my innocence by producing a tube of lip gloss. Yes, it turned out to be the dreaded grape-flavored Bonne Bell Lip Smacker. That sweet smell she was associating with pot was just lip balm. Then again, I *was* guilty of too much kissing.

Not being believed is a real emotional trigger for me. I was more upset about that than about not getting the sitcom job. I really wanted that job, and I'd been excited to audition for it. How had I given off an arrogant vibe? How could I be so disconnected from the people around me? Those questions spiraled into worse thoughts. It was horrifying to be perceived as arrogant or presumptuous. Ugh. I must be an awful person to create that impression and to be so oblivious to it. The thoughts went on and on like that. Blaming myself and only myself. The upshot is that I cried for 18 hours straight. That's right—it's not a typo. (Unless it says 180, in which case it is a typo—it should read 18.) Again, I wasn't crying about not getting the part, but about a lifetime of feeling misunderstood.

Ever cried for eighteen hours straight? I looked like someone had given me an un-facial. My face was pink and puffy. My eyes were so swollen I couldn't open them. I looked like a joint advertisement for Kleenex and NyQuil. And that's when the phone rang and I was told to come in that day to test for *Desperate Housewives*. I said, "I can't." How could I audition? I was ready to jump off a bridge, or at least a rock outcropping even higher than the one I'd faced in Sedona. I felt limp and wounded and hideous and far too embarrassed to walk into a room with most of the same ABC executives to go through the humiliation and misunderstanding all over again. So I told them I couldn't do it unless they postponed the audition. It was a risky move—what if it made them think I had even more of an attitude?—and one that could have easily lost me the part.

Was that the right thing to do, or was it self-destructive? Well, of course it would have been nice to be able to pull myself together, but that sure didn't feel like an option the moment the phone rang. If I walked into that room I had to be ready. I had to do it without sabotaging myself, without the poisonous cocktail of humiliation and anger that was still in my system like a bad hangover. As it happened, they were able to reschedule the test for a week later, and I took the opportunity to make everything right. Before I went in, I sent cookies to everyone who'd been at the sitcom audition, with a letter saying, "I don't know what your perception of that meeting was, but I was very grateful for the opportunity to audition, and I wish you good luck with the project." That made me feel better—a little "heard" and a little more in control, so by the time the *Desperate Housewives* audition rolled around, I was ready to do it in the right spirit.

As I waited my turn to meet with the producers, I watched the sun set outside the glass windows on the top floor of the ABC building and thought about how life is beautiful and full of opportunities and how, if you try, you can make it have the zen of a golf shot. Last week was horrible, but this week doesn't have to be connected to it. I had a brand-new shot, and I was going to make it good. I was determined to make sure there were no false impressions. So I went into that meeting, in jeans and a t-shirt, with no makeup on, and let them see who I really was. Not a glamorous Bond girl. Not a back-stabbing villain like the one I played in *Spy Kids*. Just me, a less-than-perfect woman and a devoted mother, closer to Susan Mayer than any other character I'd ever played.

So that worked. Deep breath. What does this all add up to? More than a jumble, I hope. What I'm trying to say is that life doesn't move in straight lines. We have lots of chances to start again if we look hard enough. We're imperfect and conflicted and puffy-eyed. We're alternately burdened and strengthened by our pasts, but we always have the power to rebound. We have another shot on the golf course. A new job. A fresh morning. A chance to ask forgiveness. Another picnic with another cliff. We may have doubts, but we control the present. We always have the choice to move forward with hope and confidence.

That's all fine and good. But getting the part didn't exactly change me. The first episode of *Desperate Housewives* was very well received. There was lots of press and buzz—everything you want for a new show. I should have been on top of the world. Instead, I found myself standing in front of one of the producers urgently clutching his sleeve. I was thinking, *Don't do this. Turn around. Teri, let go of his sleeve.* But the words came tumbling out before I could stop them. "Listen," I said, "I have to talk to you. I have no idea what I'm doing. I can't do this." Not a brilliant move, right? I'm pretty sure that Rule Number One in the book *How to Keep Your Job* is Don't Tell Your Boss You're Incapable of Doing That Job. I definitely didn't want him to fire me, but I was afraid I would fail. I know I work hard. Lots of thought and preparation goes into what I do. And I pretty much feel like I know what I'm doing (even though it took twenty years and some days I still feel like a fraud). But remember that math problem my dad thought I should rework? The lesson that taught me was that even if I was doing my best, the best that could be expected for my age and experience, it still wasn't good enough. I would lose. I would always lose. So I prepared myself for people not liking my work. This attitude is self-protective—even if the worst happens, at least I saw it coming.

Have you ever done that—told your guests, "I just threw this dinner together," or warned a tennis opponent, "I've only had a few lessons"? Even announced to your boss or anyone else that you're going to fail? Or that you're not going to meet that deadline, or make that spare, or find that secret passageway leading into the pyramid? (Hey, I don't know what you do for a living.) Well, it's a preemptive declaration. There. You've said it. You're going to fail. Now everyone has been duly notified. They may think less of you, but not less than you think of yourself. In my case, I guess I'm not the first insecure actress that producer had ever worked with, because he knew exactly what to do. He took me by the shoulders and calmly told me to repeat the following mantra every morning in front of the mirror: "I'm Teri Hatcher. The bad part is over, and only good things are to come." Great. Even more lines to memorize.

If the mirror mantras work for you, great. By all means chant away. Me, I'm not wild about gazing at myself in the mirror. Still, the producer was right. Something had to be done. I wanted to have a more positive outlook, but it's tough to uproot part of your personality. Most of us don't change our personalities on a regular basis, and I'm already at war with myself enough of the time. But every so often life presents you with an opportunity to make a real change, and if you're open and ready, you seize the day.

My fortieth birthday was a month before the Golden Globe award ceremony. To celebrate, six of my girlfriends and I went on a road trip to Napa Valley, the beautiful wine country outside San Francisco. I'd presented an award at the Emmys the year before, and in my thank-you basket, along with more luxury cosmetics than even an almost-forty-year-old actress could ever need, were a couple gift certificates. One was for a lunch at BV Vineyard, a winery and vineyard with a tasty grill in a big Craftsman house, and another was for a couple nights at the Calistoga Ranch. And so, like any self-respecting bargain-lover, I built our trip around the coupons.

It was a great weekend, and not just because we had a cake with candles and sang "Happy Birthday" to me with every meal at every restaurant. (By the time it was over I'd run out of wishes—I'd used up world peace and Emerson's health and happiness and finding true love and was down to things like wishing my dogs would stop shedding in the kitchen.) What truly made the weekend great was the company. My friends are all strong women with distinct personalities and opinions. They're bossy and outspoken and downright outraged that I don't have a boyfriend. And they aren't exactly best friends with each other. I don't mean that they don't get along, but as I looked at them all in a group like that, I realized that this wasn't a gathering of old school chums. The group was unique to me. They were my friends, and each one was here to make my weekend special. I felt a little awkward, being the center like that, but I was moved that they were there for me.

We all had adjoining rooms in the inn, and each room had a terrace and a hot tub. It was pretty decadent. Lucky for me the coupons were like the game show prizes I'd always dreamed of winning as a child. And you only turn forty once. The day of my birthday, we took a long walk up a quiet Napa road dotted with wineries. We talked and laughed and whenever my girlfriends saw a winery with the proprietor's name on it they threatened to knock on the door and set me up with him. ("How does 'Teri Hatcher Gallo' sound?" Ha ha.) Later that night, tired from the sun and the wine, I climbed into my hot tub for a soak. I lounged there, naked, lazy, and middle-aged. (Ugh. Did I just say that word? Please God, say it isn't so.) If I looked either way I could catch glimpses of my friends—one stepping out to hang a towel on her balcony, another sitting with a book and a glass of wine, a third crawling into her own hot tub. I closed my eyes, sank low in the steamy water, and let myself float. I was so content. I felt happy and complete. It was a great moment.

Then I started thinking. I was forty years old. Landmark birthdays are the perfect time to reflect on where you are and whether you have the life you want. (They're also a good time to buy people lottery tickets, which I like to give as birthday presents. Big birthdays deserve big hope. So forty lottery tickets stuffed into a fabulous purse or vase or jewelry box can be fun.) Forty is a loud reminder that time is always running out. You're halfway home. You're on the way down. Sure, when I'm sixty I'll say I had no idea what a spring chicken I was at forty. But I remember when my parents turned forty and how old I thought they were. I may not feel old inside, but I'm definitely the twelve-year-old me's definition of old. I'm biologically more or less halfway to death. It's true and it's no fun at all.

So I was thinking all this in the hot tub, and the thought that won out was that I should feel this good more of the time. We all should. We should feel relaxed, happy, and loved most of the time. But a girl can't bring six close friends to enjoy the benefits of grape-based antioxidant beverages amidst gorgeous, expansive vineyard scenery every week-end of her life. We each have to figure out how to capture that joy in our everyday lives. And that's when I started thinking about all the time I was spending planning for failure. All that time spent assuming I was going to be the worst housewife on network television. Or think-ing I was going to meet a no-good guy. Or telling myself I couldn't play ping-pong or cliff-jump or bounce off a water trampoline. Turning forty was a time to reassess, and to honestly address what I had to fix. Through the hardest years of my life—a disintegrating marriage, a stalled career, and a mortgage I couldn't afford—when I felt like I'd pretty much failed at Life 101—I always prided myself on being a great survivor. But I didn't want to spend another decade of my life preparing myself for the next disaster. I was missing out on the good stuff because I was spending all my time dwelling on the bad.

It seems like we all do this. We worry and plan and hedge our bets. To some extent this is part of building a life. It makes sense when you're young, your life isn't stable, and you're making decisions that determine your future. But as we get older, we need to start accepting and relishing where we've landed. We need to start reaping the bene-fits of the hard work that got us here (even as that hard work continues to plague us). I'm not talking about getting a built-in Jacuzzi for bliss-on-demand (though that would be nice). If you want to feel this satisfied with your life *as it is*, you have to shift your perspective. You have to spend less time doubting yourself and spend more time having hope and faith in the life you've worked so hard to create. Now is the time, no matter what decade you're facing. It's time to be a good winner.

When it comes to changing yourself there are two schools of thought. You can work from the inside, trying to understand the history of all your feelings and how you got to be the way you are. Then, eventually, you can try to use those realizations to change your life. Or you can start from the outside, acting the way you want to be, even if you don't feel it yet. Eventually it will sink in. I opted for the latter strategy. My mind is stronger than my habits. (Isn't it? Shouldn't it be?) I decided to watch for my moments of doubt, and to break the habit by sheer force of will.

Near where I live, there's a hiking trail that runs through the mountains. It's a pretty popular place, particularly among the dog-owning set, who park along our street every day. This trail was actually part of the reason I bought my house. I figured I'd have no excuse not to exercise if there was a lovely mountain walk practically in my backyard. So I got on an exercise kick recently and decided to run the trail. It's three miles long, and it's very hilly. A few of the hills are extremely long—up to a mile of gradual to steep incline without a break. Some days when I'm running up the trail, I have to stop and walk for a while. And I've noticed that whenever I do that, I start telling myself that I've failed. The whole time I'm walking, it's *God, you're so lame. You can't even make it up this hill.* But come on! Shouldn't I be complimenting myself for not sitting on the couch eating corn chips? Or congratulating myself for making it as far as I did? Or even admiring the view? I could be thinking any number of positive and healthy things, and instead I'm beating myself up. Why would I think I'd be able to walk out the front door and run three miles up big hills? That's something you have to work up to. I struggled with this, trying not to beat myself up mentally as I challenged myself physically. On the hills, I started telling myself, *You're new to this. You're not allowed to think*

bad thoughts. (At the very least, it was better than talking to myself in the mirror like that producer wanted me to do.)

Some people just run up the hill as far as they can and quit when they're tired. But if you're a searcher like me, every hill is an opportunity for self-examination. Being a searcher-type is good and bad. The good side is, we examine our behavior. *Why did I do that? What does it mean?* We judge ourselves, and we judge how we move through the world. We use this self-examination to try to better ourselves. The bad side to being a searcher is losing out on the simple pleasures that the world has to offer, and setting ourselves up for failure by judging all the time. Did I set myself up to fail by picking this hill? Or could I make it an opportunity for learning and watching myself grow? I wanted to be able to enjoy my own limitations and achievements. Lucky for me, another opportunity lay directly ahead.

The Golden Globes were approaching. I'd been nominated, and I found myself getting excited. I wasn't quite ready to imagine myself winning. But even for a pessimist-in-reform, it was still a big night. I mean, I'd never gotten recognition for my work before. (At least not since being voted Most Likely to Become a *Solid Gold* Dancer in my high school yearbook.) And possibly even more exciting was the dressing up. Emerson really liked that part, and she helped me embrace the princess aspect of the evening. I mean, whether I came home with the prince or not, at least I was going to the ball, and that was new for me.

If you get caught up in it, there can be a lot of pressure on how you look at those award ceremonies. When you walk across the red carpet, the focus is on you. You're putting yourself out there to be judged. And even if you're going to lose, which I was fully prepared to do, when they show that shot of you in the audience clapping and trying to smile graciously for whomever just beat you out, you want to look *good*. The closest thing I can compare it to is getting married. Not that an award ceremony has the love- and life-changing intensity of a wedding. But getting ready—the hair, the makeup, the dress—is a similarly massive undertaking, threatening to take away from the joy of the event if any-thing goes wrong. This was a great opportunity to try out my new op-timism and to have faith that everything would come out right.

My new stab at optimism didn't rid me of the cold-feet jitters. (Or, more appropriately, the night-before-the-ceremony nervousness.) I can't say I had a great night's sleep. I dreamt I had to save Emerson from bombs (real bombs, not the Hollywood kind). It was the worst kind of dream, but at least I didn't dream that my lipstick was the wrong color. It's nice to think that my dream-self wasn't worrying about superficial disasters or winning or losing. My dream-self seemed to get that this award ceremony wasn't the be-all and end-all. The only thing as bad as the end of the world is the actual end of the world. Anyway, I woke up relieved to be in a bomb-free zone, and instead of gathering disaster supplies, I prepared a breakfast buffet of bagels, lox, and fruit, turned on music, and lit some candles. Soon friends started arriving. I was determined to savor the moment.

Later, as my hair and makeup stylist (hereafter referred to as Miss Gorgeous) worked on my hair, he asked me if I'd prepared a speech. Ah, the speech. Hell yeah, it had occurred to me. For the last twenty years. I'd always planned to expound on how I got somewhere from nowhere, thanking the long list of people who'd helped me along the way. It was like imagining who'd weep at your funeral, but way better. Now that I was nominated, however, I couldn't bring myself to plan for actually winning. These awards are so subjective. It's not like a horse race, where the fastest horse wins fair and square. To compare different actresses in completely different roles on completely different shows isn't really meaningful. That's why the cliché that the real honor is being nominated is actually true. Just being recognized at that level for your work is a huge honor. Winning is sort of icing. But icing tastes good. (Especially when it's homemade.) Even more tasty is noncaloric guilt-free metaphoric icing. So why couldn't I enjoy it? Ad-mitting to myself that I actually wanted to win felt embarrassing. I couldn't wrangle one word into the beginnings of a speech. It made me uncomfortable—I felt ashamed for even coming near the thought. I didn't want winning to mean that other people lost. Winning felt like snatching the golden-brown, buttered toast for myself and leaving the others to take the sad, blackened end. I felt guilty. I was much more comfortable eating the burnt toast, and in this night's case, washing it down with the wine they set in the middle of the tables. And there was another part to it, which was that wanting to win would mean wanting to be validated. And admitting that I needed others to tell me I was good was even harder to stomach.

Then I realized that this was another chance (they were coming at me right and left) to change my old patterns of thought. I was forty years old. I was up for a prize and I wasn't even letting myself hope I might win. I'd spent forty years chickening out from winning and it was time to stop. We absolutely have to take time to reconsider these habits as we age. The defense mechanisms that worked for you as a kid, protecting you from disappointment, can hold you back as you get older. You have to ask yourself: What good is this habit doing me now? What is it protecting me from anyway? If you don't win a prize, do you feel better just because you never thought you had a shot? I'd just been given an exciting honor—I was a Golden Globe nominee!—but I hadn't spent a moment feeling proud or hopeful or glad for the attention. I was getting in my own way, using this habit of protecting myself instead of looking for courage and hope. Pessimism gets you nowhere.

As I finished getting ready, Emerson poked her head into the room. "Mommy, I hope you win!" she said. It takes time to end up with issues like mine that can hold you back. Kids just want things or don't want them. Their desires aren't loaded with "How dare I feel good about myself?" or "How dare I think I might be able to do something well?" In this case, Emerson just wanted me to win, plain and simple. If I did win, she wanted to know if the award could go on her bookshelf in her bedroom.

Some part of me did feel deserving that day. I certainly didn't think

I was better than anyone else. But I thought at least I deserved a shot at winning. I was tired of being a gracious loser. So I tried it out. I was a little tentative, but as Miss Gorgeous clipped extra chunks of fake hair to my head, I told myself, *It sure would be nice to win. I'd like that.*

You know what? I did win that Golden Globe, and when I did, it felt great. Actually, it felt shocking. Actually, I have no idea how it felt. I was too busy worrying about tripping, right there in front of Meryl Streep and Clint Eastwood and every actor I've ever admired my whole life, and thinking what the hell am I doing up on this stage . . . and then realizing, suddenly, that despite my newfound optimism, I still hadn't written a speech. You know that recurring dream you have where you discover that you've forgotten to write your report just as the teacher calls you up to the front of the class? Well, it felt like that, except that my "class" was fifty million TV viewers and it wasn't a dream. (At least I had a great dress, which is more than I'm usually wearing in those dreams.) My acceptance of the award and the improvised, miraculously coherent speech that went with it were a blur. I felt completely in the moment, caught in a dizzy, adrenaline-fueled whirlwind. (And if you think that just because I'm in this business it means nothing to stand near Clint Eastwood, you're dead wrong.) It was a real moment for me—not just because I won, but because I'd let myself hope for it.

And do you know how much that positive attitude had to do with me winning? *Absolutely nothing.* The votes had already been tallied and the winner's name placed in an envelope days earlier. But the point is, just shifting my attitude let me enjoy the whole experience more. Even if I hadn't won, I would have had a better time because I wasn't undermining my chances at winning in the days and hours before the event. But feeling like a loser can turn into a self-fulfilling prophecy. If you tell your boss that you suck enough times, he might actually start to believe you. (That jerk.) If you think you're going to fail, and it turns out you're right, well whoop de do. You're right. Congratulations. You've succeeded in becoming the loser you always thought you'd be. Better to behave like a winner, no matter how things turn out.

A few months after the awards I went whale watching in Mexico. My girlfriend and I and our daughters were in a small boat in the middle of the ocean when a humpback whale swam right up to us and started romancing us by swimming around and under the boat. At one point he lifted himself straight out of the water, only four feet away. He held there, a third of his body up in the air, then slowly turned toward us. We were all leaning over the edge toward him, reaching out with our hands in hope of petting him. He looked at us— looked like he was seeing our souls and memorizing them. Then he went back under and continued to swim gently around the boat. Our guide asked if anyone wanted to get in the water. This was my one chance to swim with a humpback whale, and before I could chicken out I quickly said, "Okay, I will." I put on my mask and hopped in the water with him. My mask instantly filled with water. Suddenly, I was in a massive ocean with a forty-five-foot beast, blind as a bat, and most likely surrounded by hungry, man-eating sharks. I had a panic attack. Hyperventilating, I flailed back to the boat and scrambled out of the water as fast as I could. No sooner had I taken the mask off and caught my breath than the whale swam away. I was crushed. For all my recent talk about being in the moment and believing in myself, I'd wimped out.

Then, lo and behold, the whale came back and swam alongside the boat again. Our guide couldn't believe I was being offered a second date (and she didn't even know my lousy track record with dating). But this time I wasn't as quick to the draw. I was still a little shaken, and I stalled for time. The whale swam away before I even got in the water. As I watched it go I thought to myself, *God, Teri, you just blew the chance of a lifetime—twice in a row*. The friend I was with didn't want to get in, so she wasn't failing herself. But I'd really wanted to be the person who swam with the whale, and I couldn't do it.

Then, as if in a fairy tale where wishes happen in threes, the whale came back to give me one last chance to conquer my fear. Our guide was now completely awestruck—this had never happened. I knew that if I didn't make this work I'd never forgive myself. I put on my mask and jumped in the water.

And there I was, floating four feet from a thirty-ton whale. I took a breath and held it as I dove down under water to be with the whale and feel the surge of his body swimming past me. I didn't touch him— I just watched in awe and fascination. It was even more powerful than I'd hoped. I stayed in the water several minutes with the whale until he swam away, for good this time. After I crawled back onto the boat I was so moved that I couldn't speak for half an hour. When I finally came out of my daze, I said to the guide, "Am I making too much out of this?" But she told me I wasn't exaggerating how beautiful the moment was. I couldn't believe the whale gave me as many chances as I needed. And I saw that with a little practice, and a few bonus opportunities, I really could be the person I wanted to be.

Nothing happens overnight. And you can't be your ideal self every moment of every day. But if you see something in yourself that isn't working for you, and it's keeping you from being as happy as you want to be, you can chip away at it. The results may not be instantaneous, but even changing your intentions is a powerful action. Choosing the positive just feels better.

If I sound bossy, please keep in mind, I'm saying this as much to remind myself as to tell you.

* * *

Turning forty really did have an effect on me—and it wasn't buying a convertible. (Actually, I do kind of want a convertible. But that doesn't help my point so well.) I didn't change overnight. I mean, I still fear I'm never going to find someone to love who loves me back in spite of and because of all my dark, complicated, insecure places. I tell myself that I'm too old, or that anyone who's good is already taken, or that he won't be able to deal with me having a child, or that he'll have too much baggage from an earlier marriage. I still prepared myself to not get nominated for an Emmy even though I did. And as I sat in the Shrine Auditorium watching people receive their Emmys I still had to battle that voice telling me I didn't belong.

Just a few weeks ago, Emerson and I carried out California Pizza Kitchen (uh, her choice) for lunch. Our dining room table was covered with scripts and business papers, so we decided to eat in what we call "the white living room." It's kind of a fancy room, but I don't want it to be one of those fancy rooms that people never use. So we sat on the fluffy white rug and ate our pizza over the coffee table. After a while, Emerson looked over at a side table that has my Golden Globe on it. She said, "I love looking at your Golden Globe." And then she said, "Maybe next year you'll win the Emmy." She loves that winged statue—I have to admit, it is pretty. It's so easy for Emerson to hope for my success. This time I took my cue from her. I didn't say, "No, I'm not going to win." I took a beat, then said, "Sure, maybe," and left it there.

And what about that limo ride that I promised to my friend Ned if I ever made it? Well, now, after all that's happened with *Desperate Housewives*, I know for certain that I owe him that swank ride. It's so long past due, the limo should be upgraded to a Lear jet. We still haven't done it. I blame it on Ned. He lives across the country now with a wife and two kids and a perfectly decent refrigerator, so it'd be quite a road trip for either of us. But little by little, I convince myself I'd deserve it. Maybe when I'm fifty.

It's Your Caviar, You Can Do What You Want with It

Knowing what you want and not admitting it to yourself can be tough, especially if you're a chicken like me. But it's even harder to find your authentic path when you have to contend with the pressures of family, friends, and strangers. People laugh at you, undermine your beliefs, or kindly and sincerely want something completely different for you, and it makes following your own path that much harder.

We don't start out so responsive to external forces. When I was a kid, I remember riding my bike home from seventh grade summer school one afternoon. It was a purple banana-seat one-speed that Santa was overdue to replace, and it had one of those little plastic baskets with a flower on it buckled to the handlebars. I hopped off and rolled my bike into our atrium—a sort of indoor/outdoor garden connected to the house. I put down the kickstand and heard my mom yell from the kitchen, "Teri, are you home?" I said, "Yeah . . . and you're going to kill me." She replied, "The only reason I'd kill you is if you brought home a live animal." So basically I should be long dead by now, because that's exactly what I had done, and have done many times since. Outside school I'd been suckered into adopting a kitten from a wild litter. It was orange and little and so cute . . . and, it turned out, the meanest fucking cat ever. I always suspected that I was the reason for my parents' chronic fighting, but that day there was no doubt. I was definitely the source. Neither of them wanted a cat; that much was clear. But my mom felt compelled to see my side and take pity on my nurturing instincts, so she defended me against my dad. I guess she eventually prevailed, because I kept the cat.

When we're kids, our instincts are raw and untempered by all the pros and cons and second-guessing that take over our adult lives. But we suffer the consequences. I kept the cat. Kitty was her name. (Screamingly original right?) Kitty the Terror, the biting mean wild cat that I had to keep and care for all of her very, very long life. So I got my wish, but I felt the weight of my parents' arguing and the burden of my responsibility. And that's how our simple, childish decision-making evolves to a layered complexity. That cute kitten was more than she seemed. She was (for so many years) a living thing that stimulated conflict, required care, and inspired fear in the souls of the neighborhood dogs.

Predicting consequences is part of growing up. But overpredicting and overplanning can become paralyzing. You get to the point where you forget what you want. Outside influences muddy the waters further. If the outside voices are louder than the internal voices, you have to learn to tune them out.

When I was first promoting *Lois & Clark*, I went to New York for a press junket. It was the first time I'd ever been such a significant part of promoting a show. My girlfriend, Dana, and I flew the red eye to "the Big Apple" (just letting you in on the genuine cornball level of excitement I had going at the time). My first stop on the publicity tour was the Howard Stern show. (Can you believe that? Well, I guess it was a fitting way to get my media cherry popped.) Since it started taping live at 6 A.M., they flew us from JFK airport to Manhattan in a helicopter. Okay, wow. That's just a big serious *wow*. I'm definitely not the first one to say, "Hey, let's go see everything from way up there in the sky!" I'm afraid of helicopters. They seem as fragile as insects—as if they might crash at any time, swatted from existence by some giant hand. But I did have to be on air at a certain time, and it did sound like a grand entrance for a girl who only months before was driving a Ford Probe with no air-conditioning and real old-fashioned roll-down-handle windows, so I said yes to the copter. It was a September morning, and the sun was just rising. It was so clear and breathtaking that I asked the pilot to do a circle around the Statue of Liberty—and he actually did it. Can you believe that? This has nothing to do with the point of this chapter, but I had to tell you about it because it's en route to my point. See, when an unexpected, magical moment happens, you've got to take it in, right down to the bottom of your soul. Because that's what life is about, getting to live it. So we flew around her, that tall, tall symbol of freedom, of hope, of America, and I thought about how lucky I was to be there, to share it with my friend, and to not have had to walk up the ten thousand stairs to get the same view I was seeing now. (Okay, it's really only three hundred fifty-four stairs, but at six in the morning it might as well be a mile.)

I got to Stern on time, and I think I held my own. Then Dana and I headed to the hotel to take a short break before the next set of talk shows. Talk shows are an interesting thing. I think it's a big mistake to approach them thinking people actually want to hear you talk. No one wants to hear you "talk." They want to be entertained. I've always loved the challenge and adrenaline that I get from trying to toss that comedic ball back and forth with some incredibly talented host. Anyway, we dropped our bags in the room, but it just seemed ridiculous to try to take a nap. So we went out walking and found ourselves in Central Park with hot-out-of-the-oven H&H bagels and some coffee. Then I did *Live with Regis and Kathie Lee* and *Late Show with David Letterman*. When it was all over we went to celebrate at Petrossian.

Petrossian is a one-of-a-kind Russian caviar restaurant housed in a landmark deco building in midtown. We were celebrating, so we were ready for caviar, champagne, and vodka—a level of woo-hoo-hoo that sort of reminds me of that limo ride I never took, only now I was actually doing it. So we sat down and the waiter came over with menus. Did you ever see that movie *Arthur* with Dudley Moore (one of my favorite movies)? Anyway, our waiter was the spitting image of Arthur's valet, Sir John Gielgud. (If you haven't seen *Arthur*, well, maybe you need to put this book down and go rent it to really be able to appreciate the humor of this story. But if you are miles from a video store, he's an older British man, with a dry, slow, even wit, and a deadpan expression masking loads of superior judgmental attitude.)

So we were marveling over all the caviar options and their prices. Whew, wow, them there fish eggs is expensive. But you only live once, so we chose a decent champagne to start, followed by an ounce of Beluga and martinis. Well, unbenownst to me, fancy caviar is served with as much pomp and ceremony as wine. So when the time came, Sir Gielgud presented the caviar and then lifted this utensil with a silver handle and a round, flat end like a mother-of-pearl lollipop, and handed it to me. Puzzled, I looked at him and said, "What's this?" With the aforementioned attitude and accent he said, "It's a palette." That didn't really clarify anything for me. Seeing my still dumbstruck face, he added, "It's for tasting the caviar." Well, why didn't he say so?

I scooped up a little caviar into the palette (that I now know is made of shell because silver can ruin the flavor of the caviar—as if raw fish egg flavor can be made worse than it is, anyway). I tried it and said, "Uh, yes, that's good. That'll be fine." Sir Gielgud paused for effect, then said, "I'm so relieved." Remember the accent, which compounded the sarcasm: "I'm so re-leeeeeeeved."

Then as he was pouring our champagne, I asked, "Do you think we can get some of those chopped onions and egg and capers for the caviar?" Now I've always known I was fairly simple, but at that moment I knew how white trash I really was, because he just stared blankly. Then as he lifted the champagne away and screwed it down into the ice bucket, he turned back and sneered, "It's your caviar. You can do what you want with it."

Gielgud was right. All the fanciness and rules and cultivated expectations of this world are ours to consider, accept, or reject. You really can do what you want with your life. You are presented with this choice all the time—to cave to what others want or think, or to know what you want and not be afraid to go there.

Gielgud didn't know it, but his lesson was a key one for me. One of the hardest work experiences I ever went through was the night after the Los Angeles reviews of my performance as Sally Bowles in *Cabaret*. I had been chosen by Rob Marshall and directed by him for four weeks before opening the show. It was an amazing Tony Award–winning show, with a great cast and a part that I was right for and loved. Sure, it was a risk to go from *Lois,* a moderately successful TV role, to the lead in a musical. I remember Rob telling me, "No one wants you to be good in this, but believe me, you are." Well, not according to the *LA Times* critic. I swore I wouldn't read the review, but when I heard the paper hit the door outside my rented room at 6 A.M., I just couldn't help it. The review was harsh, and I cried all day long, as I've been known to do.

I was backstage that night, only moments before my first entrance, thinking, *I can't do this. I'm humiliated. I can't do it.* Then of course I did it. I got through it, barely, and very emotionally—probably a little too much so, but, hey, that pain had to go somewhere. I had plenty of people tell me that the critic was a jerk and otherwise try to make me feel better. Then one person gave me an idea that I kept up through my entire seven-month run (which ended—I can't resist saying in case that critic sees this—with an Obie nomination for best actress). I wrote "fuck 'em" on my toes. F-u-c-k on one foot and e-m on the other. (I left the extra toes blank.) It was hidden under my tights and shoes. Sometimes I would write it in lipstick on my dressing room mirror—that was before my daughter could read. But I think the best part of it was when it was my little secret. No one saw it and I didn't show it off, but I knew it was there and it reminded me that what mattered was what *I* thought, the sincerity of my work and effort, and the support of the people around me. I couldn't let anyone take this experience away from me.

But f-u-c-k-e-m isn't written on my toes anymore, and I don't always remember to have that attitude. Not long ago I went to a birthday party at a restaurant. Miss Gorgeous (who's not just my hair and makeup guy, but a very close friend) was supposed to meet me there, but I got there first, alone. I came in, looked around the restaurant, and didn't see the birthday boy—just a few random strangers milling about. The birthday party was MIA. There I was. Girl. Alone. In bar. It was like being an insecure teenager again. I was too shy to explore. I slipped into a booth, dialed Miss Gorgeous (who was en route) and said, "Will you please stay on the phone with me until you get here, because I can't find the party and I don't know anyone here and I'm a big loser." He said, "Here's what you do. Go buy a drink, and sip it as if nothing could be more satisfying than to be drinking that drink right now." Easy for him to say. I kept him on the phone until we lost our connection, then I headed to the ladies' room for refuge. But on my way I caught a glimpse of the garden behind the restaurant. The hopping, festive, *birthday party* garden. Oh. So there it was.

The party was big and intimate, if it's possible to be both at once. Those are actually my favorite kinds of parties. There were about fifty people there, all of whom seemed to know each other except me, and there was a great live band backing people up for karaoke. One girl kept asking me if I was going to sing. I think she was assigned to this task, and after I declined she proceeded to work the room, accumulating a long list of takers. But throughout the night she kept coming up to me trying to sign me up, sort of like that whale did with the boat, but without the stinky barnacles. I kept dodging the question by talking about how great the crab dip was, but the truth was that I did want to sing, particularly when I saw that "These Boots Are Made for Walkin'" was one of the songs you could request. I love that song, and I love singing in general. But that *Cabaret* review was still haunting me. I felt too self-conscious, too worried that I'd make a fool of myself. It should have been an effortlessly fun thing to do, especially in front of strangers (and Miss Gorgeous, who had arrived at last). Who cares what they think? But it was like the cliff-jump all over again. I was afraid. Too bad that biker wasn't invited—maybe he could have given me some more encouragement. Three hours later I was still trying to get my courage up when another girl went up and sang—yes—"These Boots Are Made for Walkin'." I was bummed. I'd missed my chance— I'd feel stupid repeating a song that they'd already played. (I suppose I could have sung "These boots are *still* made for walkin'" but it just wouldn't have been the same.) It's a defeatist way to live your life— knowing you want to do something but letting your fear of what others will think if you don't do it perfectly stand in your way.

The party wasn't a total bust. If I wasn't going to sing, at least I'd take a stab at dancing. Miss Gorgeous is an amazing dancer, and I'm pretty good too. (Remember that *Solid Gold* Dancer thing from high school?) The hard part is getting my guts up to dance in public. When we first got out there I wasn't dancing freely. Dancing openly releases so many feelings: passion, laughter, sensuality, and the purest level of good clean fun. You'd think that pleasure combo would be enough to get me to dance. But, just like with the singing, I worry too much about what people are going to think. What am I afraid of? Why do I even care? But worry often dominates, and throughout the evening I had to conquer it. Being with Miss Gorgeous definitely helped.

Ultimately I let myself relax, danced for hours, and had a great time. It must've been obvious, because the next day Miss Gorgeous emailed me to say, "It was good to see you loosen up." I'd half succeeded. I'd danced the night away. But I would have liked to sing. I knew that the only thing in my way had been me.

Months later I mentioned the party to Miss Gorgeous, and before I said anything about it, he said, "I wish I'd sung something." It shocked me. Miss Gorgeous is so not that guy. Not the least bit shy and self-conscious—maybe you'd guessed that by the nickname I've given him. And so I started to wonder: How many of us at that party were too shy to sing? How many people at that party, and other parties, and in churches and at birthday parties and in our own private showers across the world are silencing ourselves, getting in our own way, missing out on fun that's practically handed to us on an hors d'oeuvre tray? And what would the world be like if those voices emerged, in a great cacophony of devil-may-care joy? Can't we teach the world to sing in perfect harmony? Okay, I'm getting a little age-of-Aquarius. But seriously, can't we do something to support each other? Can't we make the world a softer, more welcoming place?

I think about this a lot. How we should be gentle to each other, even when we're strangers. While I was working on *Lois & Clark*, I lived in Sunland, a horse community in the northeastern valley of LA that gave me the down-home rooted feeling I was looking for to counteract the glamour and stress of Hollywood. I lived there for eight years. I was living alone, sometimes working seventeen hours a day, and that's no exaggeration. I'd come home in the pitch-dark of night, collapse on my bed, and leave early in the morning. And so it came to be that sometimes I'd leave my trash cans out. Yes, I confess. I was one of those intolerable, disrespectful, thoughtless neighbors—the trash can leaver-outer. No! Not that!

At the end of one long, exhausting day, I arrived home to receive a nasty letter from a neighbor, ranting about how she had to look at my trash cans all day long, and how I had no courtesy and how could I be so rude? I guess I got her point, but I couldn't help wanting to write her back to say, "Maybe you should find a better way to spend your time than smoking cigarettes and staring out your window at my trash cans all day long." I know, I know, it brings down the neighborhood. But how about this—the next time you have a neighbor who leaves their trash cans out too long for your taste, what if you just *assume* that they are spent, busy, depressed, and in need of help, and take your lazy ass over there and move them back. Yeah, I'm a little defensive about the trash cans. I try hard to move peacefully through the world, and I'm sensitive to that kind of judgment from a stranger. If we could all spend a little time thinking people might need a little help, instead of assuming they're selfish slobs, we might live in a nicer world.

Your world is what you make of it. It's a collection of steps, one in front of the next, that form a path from your childhood to your present. Sometimes you're led against your will. Sometimes you want to stop but have to keep going. Along the way you may think you know who you are and what you want. Some elements of that may stay the same forever, and others may change every year. Regardless, you have to take ownership of your destiny and be honest about what you want, even if it's hard to admit. Even if the people around you don't think you're making the right decision.

I didn't go to my dream college—my top choices were Juilliard or Carnegie-Mellon—because my father told me he'd only pay if I studied electrical engineering. (If Juilliard has an electrical engineering program, I doubt it's very good.) My dad grew up during the Depression. All he knew was the security of work. Being an artist wouldn't guarantee me anything. My mom, who also came from a poor Depression background, had the same fears. That's why she always felt like she had to have a job. They wanted our family to feel safe. This is a mentality they were taught, and it didn't always reflect our actual circumstances. Because the truth is that there are no guarantees in life. You don't know where happiness is going to come from. I think my dad kind of gets this now. He offered to pay for me to take singing lessons—now!—as a late and sweet endorsement of the choices I've made. If only I'd taken him up on it maybe I wouldn't have been too shy to sing karaoke.

I stuck with acting in spite of the pressures from my family. But then, when *Lois & Clark* finished up, it was time for me to make another decision that was all my own. Since I was sixteen, I'd wanted to be a mother more than anything else. Psychiatrists would probably say that teenagers who want kids are trying to fix something in their lives—to have someone who loves you unconditionally and who you can control. Fine, maybe there was something true in that for me at that time. (Luckily, I didn't drop out of high school to have kids.) But one thought that had stayed with me ever since my teen years was that I didn't want to be a working mother. My mother had worked throughout my childhood. Once when she dropped me off at school, she told me that if she didn't get going she was going to be fired. My face got very serious and I let her go right away. It wasn't until days later that she realized I didn't know what it meant to be fired. I thought that if she were late to work the people at her office would set her on fire. Her work was that evil and horrifying to me. Right or wrong, having a working mom didn't work for me. I didn't like it. I was lonely. I constantly begged for siblings. And I vowed that I would give my kids a different childhood.

The working mom vs. stay-at-home mom decision. I'm cautious when I talk about this because I love and appreciate women, and I don't ever want to sit in judgment. There is no right answer in this debate. It's a struggle for all of us, and we have to make our own decisions. So much is asked of us—to work, to parent, to look a certain way, to act a certain way. I never judge a woman's choices because I actually don't think there is any easy, right way to be a woman in our society. You're not building either a career or a family. You're building a life. How it adds up, what feels right, is something only you can decide.

Becoming a mother changed my life. Previously my acting career and my marriage had been the tent poles of my life. But when Emerson Rose was born she became, at once and forever, the center of my world. I was responsible for this small, perfect being. It was up to me to protect her from danger, to introduce her to joy, and to give her the tools to build a life that will make her happy.

People in Hollywood probably thought I was making a mistake by letting my career stall in order to raise my daughter. They either thought I was finished—I was out of the game—or that it was, at most, a quick year off. (Which, of course, it wasn't.) I could have succumbed to the pressures around me, telling me I was risking my career. I still wouldn't have changed how I spent my time, but I certainly could have let myself feel torn between what people said and what I knew was right for me. But I made a choice. I ignored my agent. I didn't pay attention to the decreasing number of party lists I was on, how quickly the phone stopped ringing with job opportunities, or how the free stuff that celebrities always get stopped arriving in the mail. I didn't want to go back to that insecure hell of being an actress. Especially not now that I was a mom. I had to do what felt right to me.

Suddenly the influences of outside people fell away. I looked deeper than the opinions and reactions of my friends, family, and colleagues. A relative didn't like the name we'd chosen. Other people told me I should cut my daughter's hair. She liked to eat pats of butter, plain. People said I shouldn't, but I let her do it. I had a strong sense of how I wanted to parent, and I wasn't about to let anyone else tell me how to do it. When outside voices conflict with your heart, all you can do is try to find some temporary, tightrope-walking balance that almost works for you more than half of the time, maybe, and know that you're doing the best you can. Being a mother was a real shortcut to realizing that I could make decisions without worrying or caring what others thought.

As a new mom, I felt surges of warmth from the world. If the baby was screaming in the grocery store, people let me cut in line. (Okay, maybe they did that 'cause they were trying to get rid of us.) You know how little stores claim not to have bathrooms, but you know the employees must go to the bathroom somewhere? Well, now that I was a mother every store let me use their secret bathroom. At the airport, people who'd normally be pushing past me heedlessly stopped to help with the stroller. But being kind to strangers shouldn't be reserved for a mother with a baby. Too often we're that trash can–hating neighbor in Sunland. I took a flight on Virgin Atlantic and noticed that there was a sign on the counter that said, IT'S NOT ACCEPTABLE TO ABUSE THE STAFF OF VIRGIN ATLANTIC BECAUSE YOUR PLANE IS LATE. I said to the guy behind the counter, "That is so sad. They have to have a sign that says you can't abuse people!" Since when does freaking out at an airline employee change your flight status? You're already having a bad day. Why would you make it so that someone else has to have a crappy day too? Imagine what that guy tells his partner about you when he goes home. Seriously, people. Ease up on the airline employees! Life is hard enough.

The Christmas right after Emerson was born, I decided to make a big Christmas dinner, goose and all, for my friends and family. Emerson was only three months old; I hadn't slept in weeks. Clearly I was out of my mind to think this was a good idea. A perfectionist always, I wanted everything to be seasonal and festive. So on Christmas Eve, amidst the daze of night feedings, burping, and diaper changing, I drove to Bed Bath & Beyond to get maroon tablecloths and matching napkins. I was so out of it that I'm lucky I didn't get nabbed for an MUI (Mother Under the Influence). Nonetheless, I made it there and started wandering the aisles, haplessly searching for what I thought would be obvious items to stock for Christmas. But no, it was not so easy to find the tablecloths among the Santa Claus salt-and-pepper shakers, Marilyn Monroe tree ornaments, and reindeer-themed pleather bodysuits. (Okay, that's an exaggeration.)

I was making my way through those superwide, luxurious aisles when I heard a voice behind me say, "Well, excuuuuuse me!" I turned around to see a woman who was clearly annoyed that I'd crossed in front of her. Apparently, in my oblivion, I'd broken her shopping right-of-way code. I said, "I'm sorry, I didn't see you." She scowled at me and walked away. Now maybe this was one of those "let it go" moments, but I couldn't. I pride myself on being fair and conscious of others' feelings, and in my heart I was nowhere close to thinking I'd been rude to this woman. So, after a few minutes of stewing, and against my better judgment, I walked back up to her. I was really trying to hold back my tears, but of course I broke into sobs as I explained that I didn't even see her, and that I was a new mom, and that maybe she should just give people a little break because you never know what they might be going through. To which her lovely, generous response was, "I guess you *are* the big fucking bitch I keep reading about in the tabloids."

What a lovely way to start Christmas. I think about her, and try to give her the benefit of the doubt. Maybe she was alone on Christmas; maybe the only thing that made her feel good was being able to put down someone who seemed happier than she (and she would have to have been really bad off for an uncontrollably sobbing woman to be the happier one). In moments like this, I try to be forgiving. When someone cuts me off on the highway, instead of letting road rage take over, I tell myself that I have no idea what's going on in that other driver's world. Maybe her mother is sick. Maybe she just got fired. Maybe she's an airline employee who was brutalized by delayed travelers all day long. I imagine that we have more in common than not. I cut her some slack the way I hope others would cut me some slack on a bad day. We all suffer enough on our own. If we try to ease the suffering of those around us, who knows how the karmic echoes will lighten our loads?

We went to New York for New Year's a couple of days later. I was walking down Ninth Avenue when I saw a woman drop a full bag of groceries. It was a gray, cloudy day, and the street was full of people hurrying their separate ways, dull and unanimated. Several oranges rolled out of the woman's fallen bag; the only bright spots of color on the street. Nobody stopped to help her collect her groceries. They just walked past, oblivious. Then something happened. The clouds broke, and a double rainbow appeared. A double rainbow! In New York City! That's two more rainbows than you *ever* see in New York. They arched perfectly across the sky, right over the Chrysler Building. There was a collective gasp on the street. People pointed and smiled. Some ran into stores to buy disposable cameras. We all watched until the sky clouded over again, then went on our ways. But then the second miracle happened. The whole way down Ninth Avenue strangers stopped each other to say, "Did you see the rainbow?" and "You can still see it over on Seventh Avenue!" A twin rainbow. That's what it took to get people to notice each other, to bring them together.

Sure, you're probably thinking, *Well, that was once in a lifetime. After all, New York ain't Hawaii*. Still, rare as rainbows may be, it seemed so simple, so easy to instantaneously transform people from cold, unconcerned strangers who wouldn't help a woman chase down her oranges to members of a friendly, warm community. We're all right there, on the threshold of caring about each other, of coming together, of relishing the funny, pretty things that appear in our world. You're on that threshold with everything that happens in your life. Doing your hair. Going to the grocery store. Having a meeting. Making dinner for your family. Going on a date. Robbing a bank. (Actually, if you're a bank robber, I'm not sure any of this applies to you. Put down the book and turn yourself in.) You can find friendly faces. You can live in the moment. You can opt to be in a world that makes you smile. (Cheesy, but you know what I mean?) You can be the person who doesn't help pick up the oranges, or you can shift just slightly and turn into the person who stands in awed appreciation of all the colors in the spectrum.

I suppose you're wondering what happened to the lady with the spilled groceries? Did the rainbow awaken everyone to her plight? Come on. We're talking about New York City. What do you think happened? She picked them up and went on her way. But maybe at least the rainbow made her forget to be angry at the grocery store for not double-bagging her purchases. She was—as we all are—part of a community. We could all see the rainbow together.

Motherhood brought me a new sense of knowing what I wanted, and after that trip to New York, I started wanting to leave LA. I wanted to move to a place where I didn't have to be in a car all the time. To live in a real neighborhood in a great city. So we drove across the country and moved to New York City. I know what you're thinking—*What? You should have picked Minneapolis.* All I knew was that I wanted to make a new home and a new life with a baby. I thought New York was the answer. Little did I know that it would be the place where I hit rock bottom.

Place on Rack and Let Cool

Rock bottom. You never know how far down you are until you hit it. Near the end of my marriage, that's where I found myself. Eating burnt toast is one thing—you're unnecessarily suffering a discomfort of your own making—but *being* toast is a whole different story. When you're toast, you yourself are that burnt, useless piece of bread. You're a goner, doomed and destroyed. Ever tried to un-toast a piece of bread? When you're toast, there's no going back. The garbage can is your best and only option.

That's how it felt to me after nearly four years in New York. At my lowest of lows I called my friend Val from Chelsea Piers in New York City. It was almost Christmas, and New York was cold. The snow on the ground had long cycled past the pretty phase and was well into the gray and dirty phase. Old, foul, brown slush had melted into deep muddy puddles at every curb. If you've never experienced these "puddles," what you have to know is that they're optical illusions. Because of the snow floating on top, they look relatively solid. But when you step into them you're suddenly in a calf-deep, boot-defying puddle.

Every street corner is a cruel joke. At the same time, the invisible bottom had fallen out of my marriage. I was at my wit's end. I needed to get out, but I couldn't stand to fail. I know, this from the girl who kept a scrapbook page of her failures in high school. Couldn't I just add my marriage to the list and be done with it? But I had no tools for recovering from failure. The scrapbook that held my rejection from the San Francisco Ballet, and later letters of denial from UC Berkeley and UCLA, was some sort of self-punishment tied to perfectionism. I didn't want to disappoint my parents, my father specifically, and if I were perfect I wouldn't have to put any more letters on my failure page.

But that day on the edge of the pier, I knew I was facing a problem I couldn't solve. I couldn't stay in the marriage any longer. Yet I wasn't ready to accept failure either. I couldn't accept what divorce might do to my daughter—that I might cause her pain. There was no good option. I stood on the edge of that windy pier crying into the phone. I said to Val, "I don't know what's preventing me from just throwing myself in the Hudson." Val said, "Teri, first I want you to step away from the river." And of course I did. I couldn't imagine doing *that* to my daughter. But for a moment I'd looked down at the biggest icy puddle ever and had seen it as a haven. I knew the time had arrived. I knew the marriage was over. How had I gotten here?

Turning forty wasn't the first time it ever occurred to me that I wanted to change something about my life. But ten years earlier, when I was thirty, I thought that changes happened on the outside. They were big, concrete, physical. In order to change my attitude about jumping off a cliff I thought I had to . . . jump off a cliff. Moving across the country was meant to be a fresh start. I'd be a full-time mother. My husband, Jon, would be near the theater culture that was important to him, and I thought it would be good for all of us.

Jon, Emerson, and I took the long route to our new home—we drove across the country. We had twenty-one days, three guidebooks, and an apartment that would be clean and ready by the time we got to Manhattan. It was kind of a freewheeling trip, as every cross-country trip should be. Along with "free-wheeling," I'm pretty good at "wingin' it," so I thought I was in my element when we got to Missoula, Montana, and noticed that there were quite a few motorcyclists around. (And when I say "quite a few" I mean *thousands*.) Apparently, we were just in time for the annual Sturgis Motorcycle Rally, when about a half million bikers make their way to Sturgis, South Dakota, to converge at the mother of all motorcycle gatherings. At first we thought it was kind of cool, all those beleathered bikers escorting us down the highway. You just had to keep a careful eye on your blind spot. But then, as it got later and we started looking for a hotel, we saw the effect that the convergence of a half million bikers has on western civilization. Every hotel, bed and breakfast, and campsite from Montana to Wyoming was booked. Who knew bikers were so organized? As a last resort, we went to a 7-Eleven, planning to park there and sleep in the car. We went up to the register to ask if it was okay to stay the night in the parking lot and to offer the cashier twenty bucks for all-night access to the bathroom. But the guy took one look at Emerson, who was sleeping in my arms, and said, "You can't be sleeping in the car. Come around the corner and sleep at our place." It was one of those sweet, kindness-of-stranger gestures (he definitely didn't recognize me). And that's how I found myself lying wide awake on the floor of a stranger's apartment in the middle of Montana clutching my infant daughter in fear as my husband huddled beside me and the sound of a violent horror movie floated in from the TV in the next room. I nearly smothered Emerson, afraid that if I loosened my grip someone would steal her, and of course I didn't sleep a wink. At six in the morning we bolted, leaving a thank-you note and fifty bucks.

We hit Mount Rushmore, where it was hailing. In the middle of August. As the hail beat down on our car, the rhythm of the ice sounded like "Love Me Tender." Suddenly I had to go to Graceland.

Needless to say, it wasn't the most direct route to New York. In fact, it was exactly one thousand miles out of the way. But who hasn't wanted to throw up their arms in the middle of a hailstorm and shout, "We're going to Graceland!"?

The three books I brought on the trip were an atlas, *Fodor's USA*, and *Eat Your Way Across the U.S.A.* by Jane and Michael Stern. The last one is a guide to the most unforgettable, inexpensive, best eats across America—from pie palaces to small-town cafés. We headed to Nebraska for the best fried chicken in the country. It was a ma-and-pa place, and we got there at seven, just as they were closing. (Because that's when ma-and-pa restaurants close? Seven?) I pleaded with the "ma," of the "ma and pa," telling her, "You don't understand. We drove all the way from Los Angeles to taste your fried chicken!" She relented, and the fried chicken was really good, except it came with ambrosia salad, which I could do without. Then we went to St. Louis just for ribs.

I liked this new feeling, like I could disappear into the middle of the country. After being in the spotlight of the tabloids, and focusing on acting and appearance and glamour, that was all I wanted. Every day brought something new, and I felt myself emerging from Hollywood and coming back to being an American. I loved the vastness of America. It was so big and we were so insignificant. But that feeling started to wear out as the days went on. At the beginning of every day, Jon and I would tell ourselves, "This is gonna be a great day." But by noon we'd be fighting, and by evening we'd be exhausted. I spent at least fifty percent of the time in the backseat with my boob manipulated so Emerson could nurse while strapped into her car seat. The things we do to drive another hundred miles.

I think of the cycles of those days, how they started off hopeful, got harder as they went along, and waned to a meager close. Life can be like that. You have moments of strength and hope. Then things don't go right, you think you can't get through it, you collapse exhausted, and start again. What was missing on that trip was finding something more than sleep to build my strength. Whatever Jon and I had, it wasn't enough. By the time we got to the east coast I just wanted to be in our nice new home, where I was sure we would be rejuvenated.

We arrived at our apartment at eleven at night after twenty-one days of travel, but it wasn't the haven I had envisioned. It was filthy. A not-so-fine layer of dust covered everything. In six hours Emerson would wake up and start crawling around on the floor, so we stayed up all night cleaning. Housework definitely gives you time to think, and as I scrubbed the floor I thought, *What have I done? Why did I think this would be the solution? You can't just up and move to a new city!* Here I was in a strange place with a new baby and no idea which direction to turn when I stepped out the door. I had left behind everything that was familiar to me—from our pediatrician to my favorite cheese shop. This didn't feel like a self-reinvention. I'd driven far into the unknown and now that I was finally at a place I was supposed to call home, I was utterly lost. This was the depressing, exhausted, hopeless end to a very long day.

Turns out that being lost in Manhattan isn't so bad. The next day we had only to walk around the corner to find ourselves in a diner worthy of *Eat Your Way Across the U.S.A.* We sat in the Empire Diner having coffee and grilled cheese, and trying to keep Emerson entertained. Then we started talking to the couple sitting next to us, and it turned out that the woman lived in our building. Then the next day she dropped off a list detailing the best places in the neighborhood: dry cleaner, drugstore, fruit stand. It was a thoughtful gesture, and it was a start.

For several years living in New York, the only TV work—or significant TV work—I did was to make RadioShack commercials. I actually only sell things well if I believe in them. One of the first products I did a RadioShack ad for was a picture frame that you could record a message on. So a grandmother could press a button below a shot of her granddaughter and she'd hear Little Sally say, "Happy Mother's

Day!" Well, I thought that was brilliant and got them for everyone at Christmas.

Those RadioShack commercials were an amazing gig. They took about a week to shoot, once a year, and they gave us enough money to support our family. So when I say that I felt lucky to be a full-time mom, I am 100 percent aware that I had a kind of fortune that is very rare to come by. I turned into a New York mom, which is best captured by that moment in the middle of a freezing snowstorm when your toddler decides she can't stand wearing mittens and cries every second they're on her hands, and you have to decide whether to let her cry or have her freeze, so you say, "Fine. Don't wear your mittens," and plow that cumbersome stroller through snowy intersections while she happily waves her naked hands at disapproving strangers.

Through and in spite of the joys that came from being a mother, there was another realization nagging at me. This was a far bigger realization than deciding that I liked chopped eggs on caviar. It involved commitment, failure, and shame. More than anything it involved a child. A child whose happiness was way more important than mine. It was the looming shadow of realizing that I didn't want my marriage; that I wasn't going to be able to fix it like I did that time I put cornstarch in peach cobbler that was already in the oven. That cobbler went from runny to perfect in fifteen minutes. But my marriage? No. Ever since Emerson had been born, I'd heard people saying, "You, the parent, must be happy before you can make your child happy," and I'd think, *What are they talking about? Where is it written that you're entitled to happiness? You're the adult. Shouldn't you have to suck it up and deal with the consequences of your mistakes for the benefit of your child getting to have both her parents in the same household? Isn't having children the time when you finally abandon your "world revolves around me" attitude and focus entirely on that little baby?* Well, I thought it was. And to be perfectly honest, over the years I had watched in judgment and disgust as couples with children called it quits on their marriages in order to be "happy." I think to sit in judgment of others is a sin. If it's not, it should be, because boy did I have to eat my hat on that one.

I married a kind man who is a good father, and I am grateful for the hard-won peace we've now found. But that doesn't mean ending the marriage wasn't the hardest thing I've ever gone through. How do you accept your failure? How do you pull yourself together? How do you rebuild a life? For me that was the most difficult part. But it's also the part that taught me the most. Believe me, I'm not about to provide a fix-all recipe for un-toasting yourself. It's a long, slow process that (am I really going to milk this metaphor to its bitter end?) involves going all the way back to the bakery (that's it, done with the metaphor . . . for now). I'm still figuring it out. Sometimes I think I've succeeded. When Emerson and I spend a day collecting shells on the beach, and I feel good in a bikini, and I can still turn the head of a passing surfer, well, then I feel like I've figured out how to be a happy, successful, single mom. But other times—like when I stand in front of the mirror naked and wonder why anybody would want to be with me—I feel like I've got a long way to go.

We want to label people and situations as good or bad, right or wrong, all or nothing. The most straightforward decisions, thoughts, and emotions come when things are black and white. But after my divorce I was stuck in gray. Gray, that place where nothing is clear and all you can do is wait for the skies to break and sunlight to emerge. I'm here to tell you that sometimes the sun doesn't come out for days, weeks, months, years. It's like living in Seattle, or so I hear.

Decisions make you feel strong and in control. They mean you're moving forward. (I prove that to myself every time I reorganize my closet or the kitchen pantry.) I thought the decision to divorce would make everything more clear. But no dice. Gray skies, nothing but gray skies did I see. You can't move forward in gray. Gray makes it hard to pull yourself out of bed in the morning and drag clothes onto your body, much less come to terms with your life and your future. Maybe black is worse, but for me, gray was the new black.

After that cold New York Christmas, I came back to Los Angeles and filed for divorce. I knew I'd have to start working again, and LA was the best place for me to find jobs. The idea was that Jon would find a place nearby (which he soon did) so Emerson wouldn't be traumatized. So after four years I gave up the New York apartment and LA once again became my home. There followed many moons when I found myself on the floor of my kitchen, sobbing endlessly. I have no idea why I always ended up in the kitchen. Maybe the floor near the oven was warm? (The dog does like to curl up there when I'm baking.) Or maybe I went there looking for sustenance. The kitchen is supposed to be a nurturing, comforting place. I'd even painted all the cabinets a warm tomato-soup red. So despite the fact that there are lots of places in my house that would appear to be better sobbing locales than that floor—anywhere with carpeting, for example—for some reason the kitchen it was. Along with my decision to get out of my empty marriage and away from a husband who I felt was never around anyway were the facts: I was thirty-eight; I had a child to raise; I didn't have work or any prospect of work; and I was going to give the husband I had supported while he'd gone and done whatever he'd wanted half of the money I'd spent my whole life earning. California divorce law splits marital assets in half. The law was created to protect hardworking spouses who care for the children while the other spouse earns a living. (See how politically correct and gender-neutral I'm being? The truth is that it's a good law protecting, for the most part, stay-at-home moms who sacrifice careers and future earnings while rearing their kids. But I'd been doing the earning *and* the parenting so somehow it didn't feel fair. Now, worse than feeling like a failure (not to mention abandoned, and alone, and all those other things that seem obvious), there was an overwhelming sense of rage at having to *pay* my way out of the situation. What I thought were the best years of my life, the most lucrative years of my life, seemed over, and I had nothing to show for them. It was hard to see any light at the end of the tunnel.

I sort of hoped that deciding to divorce would instantly transform me from the walking zombie I'd become into the happy, clear-headed mother Emerson deserved. But the dissolution of the marriage left me with emotions that wouldn't dissipate overnight. As painful and seemingly endless as it was, I had to accept gray. I had to hang out in no-man's-land (literally, in my case), giving my life time and space to heal itself. That's important—let me say it again: You have to give your life time and space to heal itself. That was it. There was no other, easy answer. There's only one way to deal with gray: patience.

Being a mom is a crash course in patience. I'm a big organizer/ purger. When I'm in this gray area, it makes me feel better to clean things out and get rid of stuff. Whenever my life feels out of control I'll embark on a project, like cleaning out the medicine cabinets. When I get going on something like that, I want to keep at it until it's done. Seems reasonable, sure, but life always seems to interrupt. During my last attempt to reorganize my medicine cabinets (come on—it's at least a tiny bit more interesting than rearranging my sock drawer), Emerson wanted me to read with her instead of futzing in the bathroom. Fair enough. I told her I'd take a quick shower and then we'd read. But when I went in to take my shower, those evil bottles sucked me right back in. The next thing I knew I was at it again. I quickly tried to clean out two more drawers before Emerson noticed how long my "shower" was taking. I was surrounded by bottles and jars—shoe polish! vitamins! nose spray! oh my!—when Emerson appeared at the door. "Mommy, I want to show you something." Busted. Totally busted by my seven-year-old daughter. There she was, innocently holding out a book that explained the stars in the night sky. She wanted to read about the Pleiades. Even though the bathroom was still a wreck, of course I had to tell myself: *Stop worrying about the medicine cabinet. Be with your daughter. Read the night-sky book. Go outside and look at the stars with her.*

It's so hard to let things sit messy. To let life be messy. To live in and with the mess. But sometimes you can't figure everything out on your timetable. So you have to look for the moments when it's not so hard to tell what your choice should be. Shooting stars or aspirin? Mysteries of the galaxy or dental floss? Those are the easy ones. It's not always that simple. It takes work to not try and fix things all the time. Sometimes you just have to let it sit.

I've done a lot of baking in my life. Some of my favorites are a pecan cream-cheese cake, brownies, gingerbread, and chocolate cake. Recently, I made a cake for a Valentine's Day party. (Of course I still don't have a Valentine, but that doesn't mean I can't eat cake.) So I made this layered cake: a white layer, a red layer, a white layer, a red layer. First I put in the flour, the sugar, and the baking powder, and added butter, egg, vanilla, and food coloring. Next, I carefully mixed together all the ingredients to get a good taste and consistency. I poured the batter in a pan and baked it for thirty-two minutes. Then I pulled that perfectly risen delight out of the oven. Placed it on a rack and let it cool. You really have to let a cake cool for at least twenty minutes. Twenty minutes seems like a long time when you're sitting on a stool staring at a pan and nothing seems to be happening except that the time of your guests' arrival is getting closer and closer. Now multiply this impatience by four layers and, well, that's just way too much time to wait. So even though I put all that effort into the batter, I lost the patience to wait while it cooled and started frosting. When I saw the frosting immediately begin to melt, drip, and basically ruin my first layer, I stopped. I realized I had to wait; if I didn't, I'd ruin the whole thing, and then not only would I not have a pretty cake, I'd be stuck giving my guests the stash of red and white mints I stole from the hostess counter at a Mexican restaurant. The thing is, sometimes you just have to wait. There isn't anything you can do to accomplish something faster than it actually can be done. For me, embracing that fact has been a hard-won battle, but ultimately a freeing recognition.

If you have kids, you must know this one: You're trying to get out the door, but your four-year-old kid who's just learned to tie her shoes wants to do it all by herself. The bunny goes around the tree, into the hole, back through the hole, and the shoe should be tied. But no, now the bunny's going over to the store to pick up a few things, and before you know it he's stopping at the pub for a drink. It takes a village to tie a shoe. "I made the rabbit ears, Mommy. Now what?" Your play date is waiting at the park. Or worse, you have a doctor's appointment. You don't want to be late. You were never late to anything before you had a child. But you also want her to have a Big Girl shoe-tying moment. At this point you can be the tense, appointment-driven person who says, "We don't have time for this," and leans down and ties her kid's shoes. Or you can decide that you care about her shoe-tying moment even more than you care about being on time. If you have patience, you wait and watch while she valiantly struggles with the laces. Or, better yet, you gently transport the whole shoe-tying operation to the car. In doing so you protect your child from your frustration. You know that sometimes taking your time is the only way to do something right. As a mother, that's one thing I had down pat. I knew when to let Emerson's experience take precedence over timeliness. I have an olive green '78 Volkswagen minibus that Emerson and I love to take camping. We drive it up the coast along Route 1 and camp in the back. Of course, I've made us a comfortable nest back there. It's tricked out with Scooby-Doo curtains and the original rug—which is turquoise, gold, and brown. I added turquoise shag pillows from Target, with a matching blanket. It's stocked with vintage plastic dishes that are olive green and faux plywood around a white center. And I strung up lights with turquoise flowers around the pop-up roof. Yup, it's a groovy bus. The Partridge Family would feel right at home in it. But it has its limitations. Route 1 is one lane, and the drive up north over the mountain pass to San Luis Obispo is one long, curving, upward climb. And (just like me, I guess) the bus isn't so speedy on the hills. In fact, sometimes it seems as if even *I* could run faster than the bus, which maxes out at thirty-five miles per hour. Pedal to metal, that's all I've ever gotten out of it on a hill. Now, how would you feel driving along on a Saturday morning, getting caught behind a slowpoke like me? Well, if you're like every single other person I've ever driven in front of, you'd get pissed off right away and start tailgating in hopes that that will hurry me up. No such luck. I'm sorry to slow you down, buddy, and I'm going to pull over to let you pass as soon as there's a shoulder. But until then there's absolutely nothing I can do. This was really hard for me at first. I follow the rules, and I don't like pissing people off. But driving that car forces me to say, *I'm doing the best I can do. I'll pull over as soon as possible. But that's all I can do right now.* This lesson is reason enough to never get rid of that car, no matter what anyone says. I don't know if I'd ever found true patience with and acceptance of my limitations until I drove over that pass to San Luis Obispo at thirty-five miles per hour. It's good to find things in your life that literally and physically make you slow down, acknowledge your flaws, and stay in the gray. The fact that I'm inadvertently also teaching all those drivers behind me the same lesson is just icing (although they may have other words for it).

So I'm hanging on to patience and I'm feeling my way through the gray and I'm on the kitchen floor—but at least I'm breathing. We humans are good survivors. There's something Darwinian about our instinct to put away the bad and move forward with our lives, to still exist and breathe. Especially as mothers. We know we have to be there to take care of our kids. I knew I had to provide for Emerson. That's all that kept me going. There was no sense of a positive future ahead. My agent wasn't saying, "People think you're great. Those Radio-Shack ads have really put you back on the map. We'll definitely be able to get you back on a series." Nobody saying, "Hey, you can go be a businessperson or go back to college and get your teaching degree." I didn't know what to do. I had no marriage, a deeply diminished bank account, and no career. I'd invested nine years of my life in that marriage. All of my thirties, having so little sex that I could tell you the exact date my daughter was conceived.

I'd invested so much, and felt like I'd lost everything in the deal. Well, except Emerson—that beautiful being—and I knew deep down, through all the insecurities, that I had to be a mommy who was a good role model. So we talked about her loss, my loss, her anger, and my apology. Nothing got fixed right away, but we weren't afraid to be in it—to be right in the gray of divorce, with all the complicated feelings surrounding it.

When Emerson was four, I had gotten her a dog. A cute little shia-poo. He was white and fluffy and she named him Bluto, which you have to admit is better than naming a kitten "Kitty." Bluto was sickly when we got him, but we nursed him to good health with the help of a vet and lots of love and cuddling. We'd only had him for six weeks when we had to go out of town for the weekend. I left him with an extremely reputable trainer. Well, apparently he ate a poisonous berry that had fallen into her yard from a neighbor's tree. He got really sick and when we got back I spent a horrible night with him at the vet. I went home in the early morning when they told me that Bluto would most likely be fine. After a few hours of sleep, I tried to pull my exhausted self together and get Emerson to school when I got a call. It was the vet calling to tell me the dog had died. It wasn't the right time to break the news to Emerson. We were on our way out the door. So I used every ounce of strength to bury my feelings as I got her to school, dropped her off, and gave her that "Have a great day!" smile, knowing that there was going to be nothing great about this day at all.

I went to the vet and there was Bluto, lying dead on the table. He was still white and fluffy, but spiritless. I sobbed. I called her pediatrician, my friends, a therapist, trying to gather everyone's opinion about what to do. Some people suggested getting her the book *All Dogs Go to Heaven*. Some told me not to let her see him. Some said I should let her see him. And some told me to go get a new white dog and do the ol' switcheroo—"Boy, Bluto looks a little different after that stay at the vet." Ultimately I went with my heart. After school I took her to a park. We sat on a bench and I'm telling you, like a movie, it started to sprinkle. I told her straightaway that I had some serious news. Bluto had died—did she want to see him? She wanted to know what "dead" meant and why it had happened. I wanted to blame someone, to let that pain and sadness turn to anger instead and get it out. But I knew that wouldn't help and it wasn't the lesson. We were going to have to say good-bye to someone we loved. In a way I was lucky that she could have this experience with a dog. It's the nature of life to endure the loss of loved ones, and she was bound to have to deal with the loss of a person at some point. So we went to the vet. She cried, kissed him good-bye, and we bought an angel tombstone and buried him in the backyard.

The point of all this is that I didn't run out and get another dog. I didn't shove our painful feelings away when it might have been easier to mask that sadness with the joy of a puppy. It was better to learn that we could survive it. We could feel that pain and let it slowly drift away, always maintaining the good memories and love we'd felt for him. It was a lesson in being in that gray, yucky space, knowing that it will heal only when it's healed and you won't know it's better until the day you look back and think *I don't feel so bad today*. We didn't replace Bluto right away (later we got our beloved Pip, the Cavalier

King Charles Spaniel we still have today). We honored Bluto and the lessons he taught us. That's kind of how it went with the divorce. We stayed in the feelings and didn't force them to heal any faster than they could.

As I started getting used to my new status as a single mom, an inner strength emerged. Hard as it was to have the family unit break up, there was no looking back. All the material things we had fought over in the divorce stopped being symbols of anger as it faded away. The "silverware" went back to being spoons, forks, and knives. The "crystal" was just wineglasses. The eighteenth-century candelabra was . . . well it was still worth a lot of money and I was glad I got it!

As time passed, I realized that the important journey isn't naming the bad guy or explaining why the marriage went wrong. I'm sure I could write out a list of grievances to get you on my side. Jon could probably do the same. Any divorcée could. It's never the case that one person is without any fault. The point is that I was immobilized by pain and sadness and regret and fear and anger. I was angry every day for a year. The real journey is letting go of that anger. It's finding some forgiveness, some release. The journey is getting to the place where you can genuinely say, "It doesn't matter if I'm right. I can't live all knotted up for the rest of my life. Something has to change." The challenge isn't to keep blaming your husband or whoever's done you wrong. The challenge is to live every day being the person you want to be. The challenge is to let go.

Even in the darkest, most intense thunderstorms, there are moments when the sky clears in spots and some color radiates through. I began to see hints of blue—the promise that this gray wouldn't last the rest of my life. That encouraged me to look for more ways to break the clouds. I bought a guitar and started taking guitar lessons, trying to play easy songs like "She'll Be Coming 'Round the Mountain." I have no idea what that song really means, but it felt right. I was coming back. And then I turned my attention to my work. I had to work again. We couldn't stay in our house if I didn't, and the last thing I wanted for Emerson was a traumatic move on top of the divorce. I was going to avoid it if I could. Everything started to come back into focus. I felt creatively inspired for the first time in years. I started coming up with ideas for TV scripts and a cosmetics line. I got a deal with ABC to write a pilot, and then I got the *Desperate Housewives* part, and there was my silver lining. I already told you how I had to pull myself together to make it through the meeting with the *Desperate Housewives* executives, but I wouldn't have been able to do it at all if I hadn't come face-to-face with the storm. I knew that if I had patience and faith, the clouds would break. And when they finally did, the color that shone through was radiant.

One of the most touching things about my newfound success has been having people come up to me to say, "I'm so happy for you. You deserve it." I never thought I'd hear that. The idea that I deserve good things has never been an obvious notion to me. And the idea that I've earned my successes or that I'm a good person or that I've paid my dues—that's still hard for me to accept. I still hear my mother telling herself she didn't deserve anything. So the fact that others might think I've worked hard and deserve my success has had a big effect on me. I try to listen. If someone's handing me a nice, fresh piece of toast, I want to be able to say thank you and accept it graciously. I try to feel not just grateful, but deserving. We all are.

But here's the question: What if I hadn't gotten such a great part, a job that gave me a level of security and career confidence that I sorely needed? Such jobs are rare, and every actress knows it. If it hadn't come along when it did, could I tell such a nice story about pulling myself out of the darkness? Or would I have returned to spending much of my time in a bitter, angry heap on the kitchen floor? I can't answer that. But I know that if I hadn't challenged myself to be the person I wanted to be; if I hadn't rediscovered who I was after that divorce; if

I'd walked into that audition full of hostility and anger, I never would have gotten the part. That's not who Susan Mayer is. I can't say where I would have landed without my success. But I can say with confidence that you won't ever get offered a second chance if you don't open yourself to the possibility.

Sour Grapes Can Make a Fine Wine

Patience is the only way you can endure the gray periods. But just because the gray of divorce started to clear didn't mean I was filled with clarity and peace. It was time to start healing, and, for me, healing began at the core of my being. I had the carefully constructed nests of my home, my friends, and my VW bus; I knew how to find refuge in my surroundings. But your body is the container for your being. Shouldn't it make you happy too? Yeah, it should. Lots of parts of me got shut down during my marriage. Correct me if I'm wrong, but I think losing touch with your sexual being might be a by-product of lots of failed marriages. I'd worked so hard to salvage the relationship that I'd lost track of myself as a woman. It had been so long since I'd felt desired that I didn't know if I was desirable. I was used to burying my sexuality in order to not feel the pain of being denied. In fact, I was so insecure that I wasn't sure if I even was a sexual being anymore. I survived by turning off those switches, one by one. Now, I'm not saying I've ever had a strong hold on sexual confidence. I can't blame that entirely on my marriage. In fact, I'm aware that one of the reasons I chose the marriage that I did was so I wouldn't have to deal with that part of me, and all the complicated insecurities that came with it.

But I'm forty now, and, to be frank, I want sex. I miss sex. My friend Val told me that after I got divorced and had a bit of time to wade through the muck of the pain, she saw me start to come alive again. She said that there was a glow in my face. And she was right. I was walking around the skeleton of my house, greeting my muscles, my lungs, my heart, my stomach (actually apologizing to my stomach for all the acidy, harsh, emotional toll it had taken in the last year). I was getting acquainted with me again, turning the switches back to "on." I knew that the one switch that was going to be much harder to turn on than the rest was my sexuality. I feared it was broken. In fact, if it weren't illegal in the state of California, I might have called an "electrician."

It's crazy that all of my married friends live vicariously through their fantasized versions of my single-girl sex life, because if I thought getting divorced was going to open up an arena of endless sexcapades, I was wrong. In fact, if it's possible, I think I'm having less sex now than ever. But that's got to change. I want it to change, and when you want something badly enough, you make the effort necessary to change. Knowing you want it is the first step.

Some people think sexuality and the confidence around it comes from outer beauty, but it doesn't. It comes from the inside—from self-esteem and joy. From feeling special and, well, hot. I did not feel hot, and I'm not sure I ever have. So I started taking care of myself and my body. I took my share of candlelit baths. I indulged in fine dining. I exercised. I got a massage.

Actually, I should tell you about that massage. If you're sad and lonely and want to feel better, getting a massage seems like a nice thing to do for yourself. So there I was, lying on the table naked, enjoying my massage, while the masseur did his thing. But then he just, well, he just kept going. He *left no stone unturned*. I think he was trying to give me a happy ending! I mean, that can't be true. It wasn't that sort of place. Only it was confusing—what else could he have been doing down there? As I was lying there I couldn't figure out if I was being violated or if I was enjoying myself. I kept waiting to see if I felt one or the other—outrage or orgasm. Then suddenly it was over, and I was sort of frustrated, and you can understand why I felt more tense when I left the spa than when I went in! From then on when I went for a massage I requested a woman.

I tried to force myself to get out of the house. But sometimes, when Emerson was at her dad's and I should have been using that "free" time to see a movie with friends or go dancing, I was just too depressed. So heavy-hearted that I would just stay in my pajamas all day watching pay-per-view movies and opening a bottle of wine. Once, after a couple of glasses of that wine, I decided to embark on a more formidable project: a home bikini wax. Proceed with caution, ladies! The home bikini wax, as anyone who's tried it knows, is not for the faint of heart. And why, you may ask, didn't I have someone else do the job for me? Good question. Maybe I thought that way when I went out later to lie all alone by my pool, at least I'd look good?

Anyway, I got out my kit and set up a little lab on the bathroom floor with the strips of wax, the little heater, and a flexible-necked mirror that I got as a thank-you present when I performed in Eve Ensler's *The Vagina Monologues* (along with a baseball cap embroidered with the word "cunt" that I could never bring myself to wear). One of the monologues I performed in that show was about a woman who hates her vagina, who thinks it's ugly and just can't understand how anyone could want to be down there, let alone deeply enjoy it. Then she meets a guy who loves that part of a woman, who loves how they are all different and how you can tell so much about every woman from her vagina. He respects women and, most importantly, treasures them. This helps my monologue character understand that her vagina is beautiful and special and part of her and she begins to love it.

I related to that piece, as I think a lot of women do, only I haven't met that guy yet. Or maybe that's not true—I mean, I have been with one or two men who feel that way—but it didn't really change or fix my insecure feelings. Now, this is going to be a little graphic, but hey, we're all girls here (I think). It made me think about how when I was a young girl, really little, I would sometimes take showers with my mom. I remember being on the floor in the corner of the shower, watching my mom wash herself and getting the feeling that that area was something to hide—something to clean and otherwise disregard. I certainly didn't get the feeling that a woman's body was beautiful. In or out of the shower, I never saw my mother feeling comfortable with her sexuality. I never saw her and my father kiss or hold hands. I never saw her act lovingly toward herself, buying herself clothes or letting herself feel pretty.

So I was down there, waxing tiny sections at a time to make it less painful. It was taking forever, and it forced me to look at the reflection of my girl stuff for a significant period of time. (If you were looking for up-close and personal, honey, you got it now.) I started thinking about another piece in *The Vagina Monologues* about self-discovery in which a woman takes a class where all the women lie on mats with hand mirrors, exploring themselves. As I looked, my mind sort of drifted to this idea of femininity—of the overwhelming femaleness of the vagina— and that I have one. I'm a woman. I'm a forty-year-old woman with mistakes and yearnings and accomplishments and needs. The history of all that mixed with the bare self in that mirror, and it was somehow loaded with such complication—pride in where I've come from, what I've been able to do, and who I am, but also insecurity. I felt like that woman in the monologue, trying to accept that area as pretty or feminine or somehow attractive. I felt a mix of surprise and wonder and a strange realization that I was actually attached to this and it was me and I was it. It's not like I got it all worked out right then and there.

But on the cold tiles of the bathroom floor, I realized that I wanted Emerson to have a mother who was comfortable with her sexuality.

My small, cosmetic efforts to make myself feel better about and in my body seemed to be paying off, so I kept it up. One of my favorite beauty rituals came from a chemist who specialized in developing beauty products. She said you should never throw away leftover wine. Instead, she recommended putting it in your bathtub. It's exfoliating, and it has antioxidants.

This appeals to me on so many levels I don't know where to begin. First of all, it acknowledges the portion issue of being alone. It's so hard to cook a nice dinner for just yourself. To actually open a bottle of wine is grim, since it forces you to decide either to finish it and be a lush, or to let the extra half bottle turn to vinegar as a reminder that your romantic dinner for two was only enjoyed by one person. So if you're alone and have wine with dinner but you don't finish the bottle, you don't have to pour it down the drain. Second, I can't stand letting things go to waste. Even my brown bananas get saved in the freezer for banana bread. Sometimes the brown bananas accumulate faster than I can bake the banana bread, and my freezer is often full of black bananas frozen so hard that I have more than once contemplated better uses for them. (Like bonking the man in my life on the head. The perfect crime: All I have to do is make the banana bread and the weapon will magically disappear.) But back to the wine. I like the feeling that there's a second use for it. The wine-scented bath is much sexier and more sophisticated than, say, vanilla bubbles. It's decadent, in spite of being made of leftovers. I love it. (On the downside, my rubber duckie had to check itself into a clinic.) Now, as with the bananas, the half-bottles of wine collect in my kitchen. But instead of depressing me, they remind me to take a bath. These little things build your happiness bit by bit. They erase the harder moments of everyday living.

I found a lot of different ways to heal myself at this transitional point in my life. I turned toward the things that I knew made me happy. There's a Euphoria milk bath with white chocolate, vanilla, and white tea from Apivita. Sounds yummy, doesn't it? No calories either. And (also from Apivita) there's an Energy salt scrub with ginger, lime, and green tea. And a bubble bath from Fresh called Rice. It's sake-based and apparently the geisha used it as an all-purpose tool to detoxify. I just saw it as more alcohol in the tub. My drunken bath! But the point is that there are so many products out there that smell and feel delicious. They're not expensive, and you should indulge in a couple of them. Why? Because it's the promise of hope in a little bottle. I've even learned how to make my own bath salts, filled with hope. I give them away at Christmas. It's just Epsom salt, baking soda, dead sea salt, a tablespoon of vodka, some olive oil, and an essence of whatever feeling you'd like to have for yourself or others. Lavender, geranium, eucalyptus, patchouli, sage, sandalwood, chamomile, marjoram . . . there are endless combinations. Do those oils really give you energy or relax you or make you horny? (Did I just say horny? Oh, my. Well, it's my book. I can do what I want with it!) Who can tell? But I say use them even if they don't really help because there's a ripple effect of making you feel like you matter. You have value.

It sounds small—what's a little bubble bath going to do to change your life? But what I—and maybe other women—forget to do is to give time and space to ourselves and our bodies. We forget to attend to our smallest needs and desires. My friend Kate told me about a time she and her husband, Dave, planned to have dinner with friends. Dave said he wanted Mexican food. Kate didn't really want Mexican, but she kept her mouth shut. No big deal. She could live with a burrito. Then, when the other couple showed up, they nixed the Mexican and Dave caved in to sushi right away. Kate told me she was completely surprised. She said, "I figured it must be pretty important to Dave if he bothered to mention it. But he didn't care that much after all." What Kate realized in that instance was that Dave wasn't as wed to his preferences as she assumed, and that there actually was room for her to have an opinion. She could be assertive about what she wanted, even something as seemingly meaningless as where to have dinner. Kate's tendency was to go along with what everyone else wanted. Some people, especially men, have a much easier time just declaring what they want and going for it, while burnt toast–eating women neglect themselves in favor of peace and concord. Those small moments of self-denial add up.

Whether you're making decisions with another person or alone, the point is that if looking out for yourself doesn't come to you as easily as it does to Dave, then it takes thought and effort to be good and kind to yourself. Think of your to-do list. The bare mechanics of living can consume us. We spend so much time just trying to maintain our lives at a bare minimum. Food has to enter our mouths. Laundry has to be done. Bills need to be paid. The gas tank has to be filled. The sink has to be unclogged. But if you learned as a girl to sacrifice yourself, then your self-esteem isn't going to invent itself out of the blue. You need to work to rediscover it, to bring it out of hiding.

As a parent I've always tried to be present and aware, to spend time on the tiniest lessons and joys. It had never occurred to me to parent my own body and mind, to truly listen to my own physical thrills and grievances, to help myself emerge and grow. We spend so much time focusing on the negative, on what's wrong or missing or needs to be fixed. We dwell on the man who didn't call, the relationship that didn't work out, the chores that will never get done, and these endless worries and concerns leave us out of time to invest in ourselves.

You can find time to take just a little moment for yourself. It may seem insignificant, but it's not. When I started using body creams, I realized the benefit. It's not just the moisture that it brings to your skin. What's really important is that thirty seconds when you massage the cream into your legs. You're taking a short amount of time to say that your skin matters. *You* matter. See what products you're attracted to—their promises tell you what you need. (Apparently I need "euphoric relaxation-producing energy." Although if "good car mechanic" came in a bottle, I'd buy that one too.)

But don't take these products too seriously. I mean, how was I supposed to react when a bottle of homeopathic "Rescue Me" fluid leapt out of the medicine cabinet, cracked in the sink, and poured down the drain? I stood there watching it circle away—that mystery fluid that was supposed to save me from, I don't know, from *everything*. Did it mean there was no hope for me? Nowhere to turn? That's exactly how I was feeling when I bought it in the health food store. But it probably just meant it was time to clean out my overstocked medicine cabinet. How's that for finding the positive response? Go ahead and try to rescue yourself. The effort alone benefits you more than the product itself. And so it was that, little by little, I came back to life.

As I started to feel better, I took a trip to Vegas with Val and a couple other friends. When it came out that I'd never been to a strip club before, the group came to an immediate consensus. It was time for me to lose my strip-club virginity. And hell, I *am* forty, and I've been saying I want sex, so this seemed like as good a place as any to start. I mean not to actually *get* it, but you know, when in Rome (or Vegas) . . .

We went to a place called Olympic Garden. As we walked in, my shoes stuck to the tacky floor, and I had to tell myself it was only spilled booze. We went upstairs to where the guys were performing. Young men in cowboy hats with g-strings gyrated for bachelorette-party girls going wild. You know, maybe it just made me realize once again how deeply buried my whole sexual being was, but I couldn't find the sexiness in it. Somehow my comparative lack of excitement made me feel even more depressed. So we went downstairs to find my friend's husband. At least it would be fun to observe someone who could enjoy all this eroticism.

Back downstairs, we did find our friends enjoying the women dancing. And somehow their joy made me find joy in it too. I ordered a drink. Watched the women dance. Watched my friends watching the women dance. Watched the women dancing watching me watch my friends watch them. I wondered about the dancers' relationships with their bodies. I was lost in these musings when my friends started getting lap dances. Val's husband got her one, and then they decided I needed one too. The dancer was named Pearl. (The name Pearl made me feel old 'cause it reminded me of the TV show *Hee Haw* and I was sure she was too young to know that connection.) Pearl had a perfect body just by nature of being twenty. I sat there stiffly, trying to embrace the experience. My friends were certainly enjoying watching me try to enjoy the experience. The only rule I knew was that you weren't supposed to touch the dancers, so I had my arms tightly against my body. I didn't want to break any rules. (And I wasn't exactly as tempted as the guys around me, who were drooling on themselves.) Apparently my friends thought that watching me get lap dances was highly entertaining, because they kept buying them for me. By the second dance, Pearl had my legs apart. The third, she had her chest up by my neck and I could feel her long blond hair brush my shoulders. I worried that I'd get in trouble for having physical contact with her. I could see myself in front of the strip club jury saying, "*She* touched *me*, I swear!"

While I was getting the lap dances, it may have looked like Pearl and I were necking, but we were actually talking. I wanted to know what sexual confidence felt like, and Pearl seemed like she had it in spades. I was trying to understand if she had the same alternating layers of doubt and confidence that I have. Did she feel good, in control of her life? Was she choosing this path? She was making good money. She was working her way through college. She had a boyfriend. She was beautiful. Was that just the surface? Or did she have shame and conflict and self-doubt underneath it all?

"Sexy" has always been, to me, an exterior word—more someone else's idea of me than my own idea of myself. Just another judgment heaped on women. But it also seemed like something I want to feel inside. Here was Pearl, who clearly knew she was sexy to others. Did that feel sexy to her? We all have good hair days and bad hair days, good skin days and bad skin days, a few pounds up and a few pounds down. What could I find that was consistent enough to stay with me, to let me feel good about myself in spite of the fluctuations of my daily barometer? What could be sexy enough to drive through all of that and still exist? Had Pearl found it? Was her hair really this fabulous every day?

Four hundred dollars' worth of lap dances later, my friends finally stopped commissioning them for me. The way Val tells it, I came over with a glow of deep satisfaction on my face. They asked me how it was, and I said, "I got a great recipe for chocolate cake. I can't wait to make it." Four hundred dollars of lap dances. Val called it the most expensive recipe in the history of time.

In my struggle with sexuality, I'd convinced myself that there was an easy way to feel beautiful, confident, strong, sexual, and womanly. I just had to find it. In the protected environment of the club, Pearl seemed to have it all. She was in control. No one was violating her. She knew how to make great chocolate cake. But in truth she was selling her body. That life is a complicated recipe and for me just too mixed up with emotions between titillation and shame. For me that crossed the line. I'd been trying so hard to define sexuality as just some inner joyful right I had, without attaching it to men, money, or love. Whatever questions I had about sexuality and self-esteem, I wasn't going to find the answers there. What happened in Vegas really would stay in Vegas.

Not long after the Vegas trip, I signed up for an exercise class that uses strip-dancing moves as a workout—Sheila Kelley's "The S Factor." Don't get me wrong. I am in no way under the impression that all paths to enlightenment involve either alcoholic bathing rituals or stripping. But being naked is the ultimate state of vulnerability. It allows you to look at yourself with no interference. What better starting point to explore your sexuality?

The strip-dancing class was an eight-week course. Each class was an hour long. (I only took the course one time, but the media got completely obsessed with it. The word stripper makes everyone crazy. Cool down, boys. It's not like I have a pole permanently installed in my living room.) In the beginning of the hour, we'd lie in the dark, and the instructor would talk about loving yourself and loving your body. She'd talk about not defining your sexuality by what anyone else thought, just honoring yourself as a woman and loving yourself from within. Now for all the lack of confidence I've claimed to have, I do feel sexy and sensual sometimes. And when I'm with a man I trust, well, the sky's the limit and I can trust that about myself. I mean, I can get there. That's not really the problem.

But one particular day, the teacher guided us through an exercise to get us in touch with our bodies. She said, "Feel your legs. Feel the texture of your skin. Don't be afraid to touch your body, because it's yours." We lay there in the dark, running our hands up and down our own bodies. It got to me. As I lay there, tears rolled sideways down my face. I felt like a brick had fallen on my head. I realized I never believed I was enough. Never in shape enough, never pretty enough, never good enough at anything. (Except mothering. Motherhood was the only thing I didn't beat myself up over, and it's probably because to criticize my mothering is indirectly criticizing my daughter, which I can't stand doing.)

Maybe it sounds obvious, but I realized in that moment that my body belonged to me. Not to Hollywood. Not to my soon-to-be-ex husband. Not to the masseur whose hands got a little too adventurous. *To me*. My body was mine and I could love it. When your body is yours, it can be whatever *you* want, and you can feel however you want to feel about it. I should have loved it. I cried because I knew I didn't—I hadn't—but that I *could*. As women, we're always judged on the outside. We're fat or thin, pretty or ugly, single or married. We internalize these black and white definitions of who we are. This was the first time I had an experience where I felt like all that was taken away. I found myself thinking, *Oh my God, I can define myself, by my own standards. I don't have to wait for someone else's hands to touch me to make me feel soft and feminine. I don't have to wait for someone else to come along in order to feel good about me, to love myself.*

Gyms are brightly lit and there are mirrors everywhere. You can't help comparing yourself to other people. But here in the strip-dancing class there was no mirror. The room was dimly lit. With all those layers of external conflict stripped (pun intended) away, it was an opportunity for internal exploration. I could just be me. That was a completely new feeling. I'd been so focused on my flaws, having spent a year of my life judging my failures. Now it was time to accept myself—my flawed, late, slow-on-hills self—without focusing on my mistakes and limitations. It was time to appreciate me for me alone. It knocked everything my mother had taught me out the window.

This was the path to sexiness—finding what was good about myself in the stripped-down darkness of an empty room. Finding the reliable truths that would never fail me. I could be kind. I could read, travel, imagine. I could make the best of myself in the void that every day presented. Sexy is how you feel in your own arms. It's a state of mind, and what's most sexy is having the power to make it so. It's easiest to feel sexy in the arms of a man, when he treasures every ounce of your skin. But in the absence of that, I could find sexiness in the passion that I had for my life and what I wanted it to be and myself and who I wanted to be. I needed to make the space for that—a smooth shave, a glass of good red wine, time to relax—being sexy was exploring and being explored. It was accepting my inner self, my own fragility. The map of that exploration would guide me.

In that space, sobbing, I decided to embrace and love myself, even as I realized how much time I'd spent doing the opposite. This was my challenge and my journey. To let go of anger and fear. To break the circle of self-doubt. My career was my own, to balance as I chose with parenting. My house was my own, to paint purple if the mood struck me. It was finally time to take ownership of my body. I was blossoming now, with my body and soul. I learned a new way to walk. It's subtle—no one else probably even notices it, but I can feel it. I started leading with my hips. The way you walk changes your attitude. This new hip-leading gait adjusted my spine and made me feel vulnerable and out there, but at the same time like I was really present, experiencing things, and not hiding. You can pretend you're fine and hide behind sunglasses, baggy clothes, money. But now I was bringing my body out into the world, hips first, willing and not afraid to face myself. As my anger and sadness dissipated, I wasn't walking around in a coma, depressed and confused. I was alive. I was trying out new stripper-recommended chocolate cake recipes and rediscovering my femininity. I was letting go.

I'm Too Fried

There's a kids' book called *Caps for Sale* by Esphyr Slobodkina about a peddler who walks from village to village selling hats. He wears all of his merchandise stacked on his head, a high, teetering tower of hats.

That's the image I have in my head when I think of what it is to be a mother. Every hat is one of the responsibilities you juggle:

- *You get up, make breakfast, and pack lunches (chef hat)*
- *Drive kids to school (chauffeur hat)*
- *Drop car off at shop, pick up rental (maintenance hat)*
- *Go home and walk dog (dog-walking hat)*
- *Shower, do hair and makeup (salon hat)*
- *Go to work or manage the house, or both (professional hat)*
- *Coach the kids' tennis team (visor)*
- *Drive kids home again (mom hat—okay, I know there's no such thing as a mom hat, but there should be)*
- *Make them dinner (chef hat again)*

- *Get kids bathed, read to, tucked in (mom, mom, mom)*
- *Have sex with your husband (wife hat—or maybe a beret, depending on what his fantasies are)*
- *Then finally—you guessed it—it's time for a night cap.*

And of course, the parade of hats starts all over again the next day. Sometimes before you've even gotten out of bed to start the day, you're already thinking, *What can I do to get my head back on this pillow?* You're overscheduled, overstressed, trying to do too much. In *Caps for Sale*, the peddler with all the hats runs into trouble when he takes a nap and a bunch of monkeys steal his hats. Well, I sympathize with that peddler. Who can blame him for wanting some rest? It's tiring juggling all those hats!

I've lived my life like this, and lots of my friends have too. When my water broke with Emerson, I was in the middle of cooking dinner. I called the doctor who told me to come straight to the hospital. I asked her if I had time to blow dry my hair. She said, "What?" and I explained that I thought I looked better with my hair blown out straight, and I was afraid it would be the last time that I ever took any time for myself. So I did it. I stood there in front of the mirror, broken water and all, and blew out my hair. It did look better. And I was right. It was the last time I blew my hair dry in months. Once Emerson arrived it was all I could do to brush my teeth and shower.

It's even tougher when you're trying to do it alone. This past Labor Day weekend, in the middle of a crazy two months of shooting *Desperate Housewives*, doing press for the premiere of the second season, honoring my commitments to charities and Clairol, and solo parenting duty while my ex was away in Vancouver on a movie, I spent the weekend camping with Emerson. It was the weekend before she started second grade, and I'd promised. As much as I love getting away, it was tough for me to completely embrace the pine trees and sleeping bags when I couldn't stop anticipating the zillions of obligations that awaited me at home, but I pulled it off and Emerson had no idea how far from relaxed her marshmallow-roasting mother really was.

We started home after dinner on Monday night because I wanted to avoid traffic. I packed up the car, which is a hard-core adult production (easy, boys, not *that* kind of hard-core) involving rooftop luggage racks and the like. As you know, the van only goes thirty-five miles per hour so it was a four-hour drive back. Music would have helped me stay awake, but Emerson was asleep so I left it off. When we finally got home at midnight I let her sleep while I unpacked the car, cleaned it out, hauled our stuff upstairs, got our sleepy new puppy to do his business. Then I woke Emerson up. I hated to do it, but we'd been camping and she'd already gotten one tick, so I had to give her a shower to make sure she didn't have any more. I combed her knotted hair, got her in her pajamas, and put her in bed.

I finally climbed into bed myself. It was late, I was exhausted, and I had to be at work early the next morning. But not so fast: Emerson was awake now, asking for a tissue to blow her nose. Then a glass of water for her dry throat. Then lip balm for her sunburnt lips. It was the lip balm that nearly put me over the edge. I wanted to say, *Isn't it enough that I gave you my whole weekend? I flew a kite on the freezing beach all day, and now I have to wait on you hand, foot, and nose? Oh my God. Do you know what takes just as much effort for you as coming into my room to ask me to get you a tissue? Getting the tissue yourself!* But being a parent is a chronic condition. I knew that Emerson was extra needy and crabby because she was so tired. God knows I knew how she felt. But I was the only grown-up, so I grabbed my nurse's cap and reported for duty. Sometimes that's what motherhood is about.

All mothers exceed their limits. Sometimes I think divorced moms have more guilt and fear of failure, but I think even a married mom tends to give herself away to her kids and her husband and to put herself last. (I mean, obviously I believe that—see the title of this book.) When you push too far, there are real consequences. There was a time when I was working, shooting many days in a row, and really exhausted. That weekend I had a long-term plan to take my daughter to Disneyland for a playdate with our friends (and all the characters, from Alice to Eeyore). Friday night work went until 10 P.M. and then we made the late-night drive to Disneyland. I awoke in the hotel at 1 A.M. with the most painful migraine I've ever had. Lots of people get migraines from chocolate or red wine. Me, I get them from exhaustion. This one was a doozy—a vise-screwing-my-head-so-tightly-that-it-felt-like-whatever-post-mothering-brain-cells-were-left-might-ooze-out-my-ears kind of doozy. I couldn't move or think, and as the hours of this second-by-second torture added up, I considered throwing myself off the balcony and taking up ghostly residence at the Haunted Mansion. Of course I didn't do that, but I did (later, when my brain was my own again) come to understand why people with chronic pain consider ending it all. When you're in it, you just can't believe that you can survive the pain for one more second.

I was alone with Emerson, and I didn't want to disturb her, so I writhed in silent anguish for five hours, crying as quietly as I could. When she woke up, bless her heart, she went through every bag looking for medicine that might help. She tried to get ice out of the refrigerator but there was none, so she brought me a cold cloth and held me. That helped a bit, but brought up all my stuff from being a child who took care of her mother. I didn't want Emerson to feel responsible for me. Nor did I want to bother anyone (yes, if I had a shrink, we'd address that in our next session). Finally, at around 10 A.M., my girlfriend arrived bearing Motrin and ice and swooped my daughter away. The headache started to subside, and I slept while they rode all the rides I had imagined taking Emerson on for the past year. I missed seeing that shot of courage it took for her to go on Space Mountain and the Matterhorn for the first time. I missed the laughter and joy of sharing popcorn and caramel apples. And the next day I went through the motions of riding some with her, putting on a happiest-place-on-Earth smile while the evil migraine tapped at the window of my brain with a long, crooked finger, saying, *You sure you want to do that? I'm right here, waiting for you.*

You try to survive as best you can, and sometimes you're proud just to make it back to bed. But you can't let every day be about what you have to get done that day. Even if you manage to check everything off the list, does that make it a good day? Really? Or is it just a step forward on the treadmill that is constantly trying to carry you backward? Isn't it hard to feel like you're living your life when you're just doing what it takes to get by? "Getting by" isn't a life. "Getting by" is when you're most likely to grab whatever pops out of the toaster oven and shove it in your mouth as you herd the kids into the car without giving a thought to your own needs and your own satisfaction. You're so focused on what needs to get done that you lose track of who you are. Forget not seeing the forest for the trees. You're not seeing the forest because who has time for a friggin' hike?

You need to find a way to preserve yourself. You have to take care of yourself at the same time you take care of others. You have to really live and accomplish your life. If you don't, you'll be eating the burnt toast. (I know, enough with the toast, but it *is* the title.) Accepting less than you deserve has three bad results. First, you're sending the wrong message to your kids. You're at once spoiling them and teaching them that one day, like you, they'll have to set their basic needs aside. That's right—they'll be too selfish now and too selfless later. Second, you're damaging your own self-esteem. You'll never find inner contentment if you're constantly denying yourself. Finally, if you're always self-sacrificing, your kids won't see you as deserving of comfort and fulfillment. And boy will you regret that when they pick your nursing home and never visit you there and you're left playing digital bingo against a cyborg nurse (they'll definitely have cyborg nurses by the time we get there). So how do you stop eating that toast? How do you balance being a mother and taking care of yourself?

Always accommodating your kids can be as bad for them as never accommodating them. Take a little thing, like the music you listen to in the car (when they're awake). Maybe you figure the kids' music keeps them entertained and isn't such a big sacrifice for you to make. But you end up playing Britney Spears until you contemplate bleaching your hair. Your inner pop music protective shield is wearing down, and the next thing you know you're angry, exhausted, feeling empty, and thinking you need a big glass of wine as soon as the kids are in bed. You haven't fed your own soul. I try to let Emerson see that it's my life too. Luckily, Emerson prefers show tunes like *Guys and Dolls*, *Wicked*, and *42nd Street* to Britney Spears. But let's face it. There are only so many times a person can hear "Lullaby of Broadway" before she loses her mind. So when we're on a driving trip, I make it very clear to Emerson that we're going to take turns listening to her music, then mine. She knows that we'll switch, and she knows it will be fair. It's always been this way, and we're both satisfied with the arrangement. Plus, kids are in the process of forming their musical tastes, so go ahead, introduce them to everything from Abba to Zeppelin.

It's the same thing with eating. What are you going to have for dinner? If you leave it up to the kids, it's the same old macaroni and cheese every single night—occasionally broken up by cheese and macaroni. What if you feel like having grilled salmon, vegetables, and wild rice? I say put it in front of them. Say, "This is what we eat in this family." They'll eat it. Maybe not the first night, but eventually. Just remember, if you don't show them that you value yourself, what message are you giving them? For now, you're telling them that their needs are more important than other people's. And when they grow up to be parents, they'll feel like they should give themselves away. I'm not making excuses to be a selfish mother. Selfishness requires acting without thinking of others. What I'm talking about is, ultimately, the opposite. You're not just making on-the-spot decisions about what will get you through dinnertime. You're making a life.

Note that burnt toast can pop up out of nowhere. Emerson and her father were scheduled to go on a short vacation to an east coast beach. My daughter is well traveled. She's been to Portugal with me for a charity event; Mexico and Hawaii for vacations; and most recently on safari in Africa. But all those trips were with me. We've spent time apart—I've left her with her dad for a few days when I had to work out of town—but she's never gone and flown off on a jet plane, leaving me behind. She knew it was coming up. I knew it was coming up. It was going to be the first time she'd leave me to have her own adventure.

Emerson loves her dad, and sees him regularly here in LA. He's great with her, and he'd planned a fun trip. So I never would have anticipated what happened the day before she left. Emerson and I were hanging out in my trailer between takes of *Desperate Housewives*, coloring and eating fudgesicles in the 102-degree heat. I'd gotten everything packed up for her trip the night before.

Then it came time for her to leave the set and go to her dad's, where she was to spend the night before leaving on an early plane. But she just wouldn't go. She cried and hugged me, sat in my lap, kissed me. Little kid tears streamed down her cheeks as she told me over and over that she'd miss me and that she loved me. She kept saying that: "I love you, Mommy." It took everything in me not to say, "Oh, honey, it's okay. You don't have to go if you don't want to." In fact, I was so close to caving that I leaned over to my makeup artist and whispered in his ear, "I can't say she doesn't have to go, can I?" He wagged a mascara wand at me scoldingly: No! I knew he was right. So I let her be tugged away. She ran back to me and asked for my shirt. She said she wanted something with Mommy smell on it. So right there in front of everyone I took it off (wardrobe's still looking for it) and gave it to her. It soothed her a bit, though the tears were still there as she and the nanny drove away. My friends at work consoled me and I resisted crying—I didn't want to ruin my mascara, especially after the solid advice my makeup artist had given me—but that afternoon was torture.

The next day I was back at work early. While I was filming, I got a message that they had landed and everything was great. Emerson was happy. No problems at all. Yippee!—I had done the right thing, encouraging her to go. After a long day on set, I arrived home, hungry and tired, only to find that the new puppy had pooped and peed all over the kitchen. I guess he had his own separation anxiety. *Nice*, I thought, *Well, better clean that up, no one else will. No one else will.* It wasn't a big mental leap from there to: *Hmmm, I'm alone. I'm alone and I'm lonely.* My daughter, the love of my life, was off having a wonderful time. Now that I had the free time I sometimes longed for, I couldn't handle it. While she was building sand castles and a relationship with her dad, I was cleaning up poop and mindlessly wandering the empty house not sure what to do with myself. My Responsible Mother Mode clicked off. I didn't have to feed her, put her to bed, lock up the house. I knew I was supposed to be enjoying that freedom. But sometimes, when the responsible mother is off duty, it seems like there isn't much of a person left in her place. Being a mother gives me such clear purpose and definition in and for my life. I'm so important to her, and I feel pretty confident about the job I'm doing. But that confidence and sense of self-importance is dependent upon having someone to mother. It doesn't stretch into other parts of my life. When Emerson's gone I'm suddenly hatless—and the cold air is sharp and unexpected. Loneliness washes over me and I get depressed. Opening and closing the pantry, trying to decide if thin mint cookies would make me feel better or worse. This was not right. I needed a new perspective. And maybe a thin mint cookie. But mostly, a new perspective.

We spend so much time struggling with the great balancing act of mothering. Now I had a chance to take a much-needed break. But I was like a cocktail waitress who's had a drink grabbed off the corner of her tray. She has less to carry, but she's so unprepared for the change in balance that she drops the whole tray. I needed to get a life. I needed to have something of my own to serve as ballast, to fill me up, so that I never relied too heavily on her to give me a reason for being. I mean, I've always been aware of this—and I've gone to lengths to make sure she feels no responsibility for my happiness and fulfillment. But I had to be honest: In that moment, when she was gone, I felt completely empty.

When this happens, I hide away in there, lick my wounds, and try to get control before I can emerge—like a groundhog waiting until the clouds have passed and then poking his head out to see if it's all okay. Without Emerson I have no reason to go in the family room. I don't eat at the dining room table. Rooms lose their usefulness. The space beyond the kitchen and my bedroom feels cavernous, looming too big for me and my thoughts. When life is busy and noisy with kids and work, that inner melancholy is drowned out. But when the house is quiet and still, I remember that I have no one to share it with. I can't help reflecting on my life, where I am, how I got here, and what's missing.

I knew what sort of thing I should be doing. It would be nice to go to Pace, one of my favorite restaurants, for dinner. I could have one of their pastas, or the steak, or the chopped salad. But I didn't want to go alone. What about calling my married friends? I imagined the conversations. They were just sitting down to a family dinner. They were having another couple over. They had exactly four steaks sizzling on the grill. I could practically smell them. Why bother to make the phone calls? The dialogue had already happened in my head and left me with nothing.

This is the curse of being a single mother. It's too sad to hang out with your married friends who have kids when your kid is away. You don't have any single friends. It's too pathetic to go to a bar alone— what are you going to do there? I mean, you can't sludge through the standard lines: "I grew up in . . ." or "I used to like red wine but the sulfurs are bugging me so I switched to white." It's enough to send you running for an online dating service, but your husband got the computer so you settle for Starbucks. You don't even like coffee. So I just go straight to that purple haven I call a bedroom, lock the door, turn on the fireplace (it's electric—less chance of fire), light candles (so much for fire safety), and sulk. If I'm lucky, I'll find a project—last Saturday I spent ten hours sitting on the floor of my bedroom watching *In Good Company* and *Mystic River* and *Saturday Night Live* while painting t-shirts for a charity event. I never left the room. That's depressing. That's my life.

When Emerson came home from her trip with her dad, she was just beaming. She looked like she'd grown five inches. She was abuzz with stories about making new friends, going on rides at the boardwalk, and building amazing sand castles. She had flown back and forth across the country without me, no problem, and was feeling 100 percent terrific. So while the needy insecure part of me was struggling inside with thoughts of *You mean you didn't miss me? You didn't wake in the middle of the night yelling "Mommy"?* the bigger part of me, the better part of me, the part of me that had spent those past four days coming to terms with my own life, was wise enough to remind myself of two things. First, that the right thing to be thinking was, *What a good job I've done. My daughter feels love, feels consistency, feels comfortable enough in her environment to go experience independence. Yup, I'm an excellent mother.* Second, that the right thing to be doing was getting more of a life independent from her. Because she's starting to get one away from me, and that's exactly the way it should be.

When Emerson took her trip and I had my lonely four days, I realized I had to stop feeling hurt by her ability to live without me and to start feeling proud of it. I had to stop feeling depressed at the emptiness of my life and to start making good use of it. It's good to be attached to your children. But there's a line where love crosses over into dependence. Every mother has to keep an eye on this. When they're infants they need us so desperately, twenty-four hours a day. But as they age we have to actively modify our behavior, so that we can reclaim our lives as they become available to us. We spend so much time focused on our children that our identities get wrapped up in theirs. We need them to need us. But in the face of all the work and time and hats, the best way for us to weather their changes, and to let them grow up, is to keep track of who *we* are. We need to remember ourselves not just as mothers, but as women. That's how to be the best you and the best mom.

So remember to give and take. Society's good at asking us to give, give, give. Drive the carpool. Lead the Girl Scout troop. Handmake a costume for the school play. Cook dinner for your husband. Everyone's asking for something from you. Whether you're happily married or divorced or a single parent by choice, you need and deserve adult time. You need to teach her how to put a slice of bread in the toaster, wait for it to brown to perfection, pull it out, and enjoy it. You need to show her that if you're distracted and the toast gets burnt, you'll try it again because you're worth it. You value yourself, your body, your satisfaction in life as an adult and as a woman. You need to show her that you know how to take, take, take what you deserve. That's the best way to teach your children to value themselves. Okay, now I'll take off my preacher's hat.

Recipe for Disaster

Let's be honest. Isn't there one thing—just one thing—in your house that you're terrified will get destroyed? Maybe it's a wedding present, a gift from a loved one, or a family heirloom? Perhaps that wooden table that's survived all these years without a single water ring? There's always something. In the midst of festivities, you're always a little bit aware of it. What if it got broken? Then what? How quickly would your laissez-faire attitude disappear if you had to witness your favorite vase shattering into tiny fragments on the living room floor? Would you burst into tears? Throw a fit? End the party? Would you pretend it was no big deal until your guests were gone, then spend hours on the floor, trying desperately to reassemble the jigsaw puzzle of shattered pieces?

After Hurricane Katrina, there was a piece in the *New Yorker* about a family who couldn't afford to leave New Orleans and wound up spending four days on their roof. When they were finally rescued, their house and everything in it gone forever, the grandmother said, "I had a wineglass I really liked . . . even that's gone." The older we get, the more our stuff comes to hold meaning. We become emotionally attached to it. And so, over time, these treasures are worth more than their actual value. They represent pieces of our lives. Even in the midst of holiday parties or devastating hurricanes, we can't help but have one eye on that most precious thing. To lose it is unimaginable. It would be heartbreaking. Or would it?

Just before the Golden Globes, Diane Sawyer came to interview me in my house for *Primetime Live*. This was huge. It was the first big thing to happen in the year of crazy surreal change that accompanied the success of *Desperate Housewives*. Diane Sawyer was going to be in my house! While I was still at work, a camera crew came to set up the living room. I hadn't really thought about what might be involved, but when I walked into the house, I gasped. The place was barely recognizable. Everything in my entire living room had been moved to make room for five huge cameras. I guess that's what they needed to do to capture my "reality." There were lights and monitors and sound people everywhere. No problem; a little rearranging. But the first thing I thought when I walked into that room was, *Where's the Kaiser woman?*

When I was eleven, my mother left me and my father for three months to work in Europe. It was a painful separation. As I'm sure some of you remember, being a preteen girl is very intense. You're changing so fast that every little thing seems critical: your clothes, your hair, what earrings you wear. It all takes on heightened meaning, like the world will fall apart if you don't figure out the mysteries of the mall. Were my feet too big? Were my eyebrows growing together into the dreaded unibrow? Was it time to start shaving my legs? Those were questions my dad couldn't answer, as they didn't involve integral and differential calculus, and I had nowhere else to turn. I had no sisters or aunts to reach out to. My parents and I led a pretty tight, isolated life. For all her mixed messages, I needed my mother.

After what seemed like a lifetime to an eleven-year-old, she finally returned from her trip. One thing she brought back with her was a beautiful white Kaiser porcelain figure of a nude woman. She sits in a graceful yogic pose, with one foot planted on the ground, knee up, the other leg curled under. I always associated the figurine with that tough time when my mother was gone. But I was also captivated by her. That nude woman watched me go through my teen years, and came to represent a confident sexuality and feminine mystique that was otherwise missing in my life at the time. I think that's why this sculpture has always been stunning to me. Her toes and fingers are so dainty, so graceful, so specific. She embodies the ease I wish I felt in myself as a woman. So she was a loaded figure(ine) for me. Full of what I missed, and wanted, and yearned to be. Three years ago I asked my mother if I could have her, and she's held a place of honor in my living room ever since.

Now where was she? Trying not to freak out, I clambered through the new obstacle course of the living room searching for her. And then I saw her—safely tucked away in a corner. *Phew*. For a moment I contemplated stowing her away upstairs, but then I decided I was being ridiculous. These people were professionals. They did this all the time. I could trust them. I'm laid back. Yup, that's me. Totally laid back.

The interview was long and nerve-wracking. I was most nervous when—God knows why I said I'd do this—I made chocolate chip cookies from scratch. I've done it thousands of times, but never on camera with Diane Sawyer watching my every move and simultaneously asking me what it was like to get divorced. You know, the easy questions. I was trying to answer her honestly, without hurting my daughter or my ex, and in a way I wouldn't regret forever. At the same time I was busy making sure I had the sugar, not the salt, and imagining myself pulling out burnt cookies for a national audience who would forever believe that I had no homemaking skills and I was a big fake of a mother. My hands were shaking as I poured the ingredients, so I had to worry about how that would look on top of everything else.

I could just see the tabloids: "Teri Hatcher has old lady hands." (Just watch, even that joke will make it into the tabloids as my latest cosmetic woe.) I have to digress to say that while I was juggling all that, I thought it was a perfect example of how mothers try to wear too many hats. We're baking and working and talking and shaking from the effort of it all and just hoping that it works out for the best, that nobody sees through our façade of confidence and that nobody judges us as incompetent. Well, thankfully, the cookies did come out. (Later, Diane told me she brought one home for her husband Mike Nichols and he loved it. That was a huge deal for me—Mike Nichols liked my cookie!)

Anyway, after a long, emotional day we wrapped up the interview. I said good-bye to Ms. Sawyer, and settled down to finish my glass of wine, feeling pretty proud of myself. The crew was in the living room, packing up and carefully moving the furniture back where it belonged. Then one of the producers came into the kitchen looking distraught. He said, "Something doesn't look right." I saw his face and thought, *Please don't let it be the porcelain woman.* But of course it was. Yes, of all the furniture and art and fragile things hanging out in my living room just waiting to be destroyed, all those things that I would hardly have cared about at all, it was the porcelain woman that had broken. "Something doesn't look right" was a bit of an understatement. They had knocked her over, and one of her sensual, graceful, feminine legs was now broken off from the rest of her body.

I sat down, breathing hard and suppressing tears, but I didn't fall apart. I could get really mad, and at another point in my life I probably would have. But I didn't. Instead, I tried to understand why my most important possession had been the one to get broken. Why the one and only thing that mattered? It had to mean something. But what? The crew tried their best to comfort me, saying, "It must mean you're going to win the Golden Globe." That wasn't exactly the deep meaning I was looking for.

Then I thought about how I had just reacted. Instead of freaking out like I would have ten years ago, I was taking a deep breath and looking for the lesson in the moment. That alone was something to take away from this. I liked that change in myself. It definitely came from motherhood. Would I want Emerson to yell at people when something went wrong? Never. I wanted her to learn that if you can pause and reflect on a situation before reacting, a world of options spreads before you. Now I had internalized that lesson. Everything that happens—good, bad, win, lose—is an opportunity for enlightenment. I had the option of making the people responsible feel better or worse. I chose to make them feel better.

I looked up from the chair at the concerned faces around me and smiled to show that it was all right, but then I realized that it went deeper than that. That figurine was loaded with emotion and history. It was full of pain and love and hope and inspiration, and now it was gone. I felt a surprising sense of liberation. All the memories and emotions I had attached to it were now free-floating. They were out there in orbit, available for me to catch and carry forward or to release forever. This was my chance to examine them, to decide what I wanted to keep and what I wanted to leave behind. And so I did. I took the inspiration of her sensuality, her confidence, her graceful poise and kept them for myself. And I let the pain of what was missing in my childhood float off into the ether.

The Kaiser woman was broken. This was a moment I had never wanted to happen. But now that it was upon me, I felt a sense of enlightenment. Objects are important; over time we form emotional relationships with physical things and attach meaning and value to them. When something breaks, the first way we try to make ourselves feel better is to say, "It's just stuff. It doesn't matter."

But I think we can look at it differently. Things are not just inanimate objects. They're experiences. You have them for as long as you have them, and they represent that passage of time in your life. It's not so much the fact that they break that's important. It's the experience of that ending. It's how you react and how you recover. If you can see the good in it, if you can find the liberation in not having it anymore, then the broken thing isn't lost forever. It stays with you in the form of that experience. Sometimes that end, that freedom, holds the greatest lesson of all.

Think about it in terms of relationships. When they fall to pieces, and your heart shatters, it feels like something's been lost forever. It takes me forever to go on a date with someone, and then it takes even longer to get to the point where I sleep with them. That's a scary, intimate step for me, and you know what? I'm fine with that. For me, sex can't be recreational. So, recently, I finally got to that level with a guy. I liked this guy. And let me say again how hard it is for me to open up to anyone. It's a tricky arena for me, especially now—he has to understand my strange celebrity life; he has to appreciate the importance of my relationship with my daughter; he has to have a full and interesting life and be comfortable with his own success; he has to be smart, witty, thoughtful, and fun. Those guys aren't a dime a dozen, and among them I still need to find one who likes me.

So I found one, yippee, and can I just say—it was all amazing. I'm talking life-changing, fear-releasing, sex-like-I've-never-had-in-my-life amazing. It was deep conversations about religion, politics, philosophy, even cappuccinos. Everything this girl wants.

And then the torture began. The compulsive calls to check my answering machine messages. The feeling of not wanting to take a shower or play music too loudly lest I not hear the phone ring. Leaving the ringer on all night (which I never do) just in case he decided to call at 3 A.M. And the absolute worst—staying home alone night after night when I could be out with friends or at a movie to do nothing but watch that stupid phone not ring.

Boy, when I mentioned earlier that I can go down the rabbit hole of despair, did I say I could build a fort and a self-sustaining dystopia down there too?

I think of that scene in *Tootsie*, one of my favorite movies, where Teri Garr's character, after sleeping with her friend (played by Dustin Hoffman), says something like, "Michael, I know there is pain in every relationship. I would just like to have my pain now, okay? I mean, otherwise I'll just wait by the phone, and if you don't call then I'll have pain and wait by the phone." Well, that's me all right. I sleep with a guy and then wait for the pain. That quality has got to go.

So what does a girl do after so many sobbing, sleepless nights, waiting for the guy she thought was Mr. Right to call? How can it be that it was everything I wanted but nothing he wanted? How can I be experiencing the greatest connection of my life, something I've never experienced with anyone else, while he's, well . . . not calling back. And I'll never know why, because at least I have the self-respect to not call him, unless I happen to be delirious with a fever and high on cough syrup. (Okay, I did it. I did the Bad Thing of calling and asking if we were ever going to see each other again, only to face a long, uncomfortable silence ending with, "I gotta go. I'll call ya." Yeah right.)

What does a girl do? If she's anything like me she keeps checking her answering machine more times in a day than she washes her hands. And each time she hears, "You have no new messages," she cries. And cries. And, well, cries. Lucky for me I can't cry forever. I cannot work with a swollen fish face, so I'm forced to stop if for nothing but vanity. Even when the tears were gone, I still felt broken, the fragments of my heart scattered around me like that shattered figurine.

But, as with the figurine, we have choices about how we react when things break. And I realized that those pieces weren't hope, exactly. They were more like power—the power I'd given to this man in the form of vulnerability. Now I wanted it back. The first step to getting your power back is realizing you gave it away. Well, I did with this guy. He didn't ask for it. But I gave it to him anyway. I wanted to take that risk. I wanted to be vulnerable. Now I had to pick up my broken heart pieces. I figured it'd be nice to have my heart in one piece for at least another forty years.

I was enduring another herb tea–infused failure of an effort to sleep peacefully when it dawned on me (and yes, it was almost dawn) that I should visualize where I'd left my power. So I pictured my power in red velvet bags, sort of cinched closed like that old-fashioned Gold Mine gum that came in little nuggets stuffed in drawstring sacks. Once I got a clear image of what my power looked like, I went around gathering it up. I pictured me and him and all the places where I gave away (or left) those gold nuggets of power. I politely asked for it back as I saw it lying under the crumpled white sheets of his bed, on his couch, in the jacuzzi, on the wooden counter of the kitchen. Hell, I even went back to the movie theater where we made out and asked him to give me back my power there too. So there I was at the end of this long meditation, my arms loaded with so many bags of my power that I could hardly hold them all. And you know what? It worked. As dawn broke, I finally fell asleep.

When I woke up I felt better, and I still feel better, and now that my power was intact, I felt okay about the journey. I was able to see the experience as worthwhile, even if it was over. It's part of that burnt toast thing—if you let go of all that power for good, it's another way of saying you don't deserve to be happy, you aren't worth his time, he was right to blow you off. So you should look to take your power back. Find where you lost it. Maybe it's not under a guy's sheets. Maybe it's at your office or in the bank or with your neighbor . . . Picture what yours looks like—it could be a gold coin, pink quartz crystal, a little black chunk of coal that keeps your engine going—just come up with an image and gather it all back up.

It feels good to get your power back. You may still have the emotional pain from the rejection or disappointment, but at least you're making your own choice about how to get through. I won't be able to forget how much of my heart I gave to that guy, and it hurts to not be able to give him more, but when I have all my little red satchels collected in neat rows, I can remember the good parts and feel strong enough to weather the pain.

All this is part of life. We lose things that we treasure. Jobs end. Relationships fall apart. Children grow up and leave. Houses burn to the ground. As much as you give importance to things that you love and treasure, you can still let go of them. You can still be a whole person. It's empowering.

You can imagine how Diane Sawyer's crew dealt with my little statuette. They sent it to a curator from the Met, who repaired it as if he were piecing together a priceless antiquity. Meanwhile, a friend found me another one. No, not on eBay, though of course we looked. He found it somewhere in England. The two Kaiser twins arrived at almost the same time, both in great condition. They're handmade, so they're slightly different from each other. But they migrate around my living room and feel to me like dainty, sensuous bookends suspending between them the narrative of my relationship with them. Damage and healing. Pain and love. A beginning and an ending. A complete story.

$\mathcal{W}hat\ is\ the$ meaning of the stuff in our lives? How does it come and go? What are the lessons? Is it a burden or a reward? My designer-friend would kill me if she saw the drum set I've squished into the middle of the carefully planned living room. Or the picture of Ray Charles that I hung on the wall. But I got that drum set at a charity auction. It's signed by Van Halen. Emerson rocks out on it, and it makes me happy. You just have to know yourself. Know that you can't do anything wrong so long as it's an extension of yourself . . . and it's not against the laws of the land. And live in it. Feel free to steal my mantra: *It's a home, not a museum!* Live in your house!

There's a difference between appreciating things and owning them. I explain this to Emerson when she plays with a toy at school or at a friend's house and wants it for herself. Just because she appreciates it doesn't mean she has to own it. I do the same thing when I see something expensive in a store, like a beautiful coat. I remind myself that just because I admire the design doesn't mean it has to be in my closet, making me feel guilty every time I don't wear it. When I'm in a museum, I appreciate the art with no intent to buy. But my house is the opposite. I own it. I don't keep plastic over fancy things. I don't forbid Emerson to go in certain rooms. I don't "save" my house for something else, some other part of life. This is my life. Don't get me wrong. I'll gladly Scotchgard the crap out of every fiber of that fluffy white rug. But crayon on the couch is a lasting memory of a kid's youth. If it happens, it happens. I'm not about to terrorize Emerson if she winds up doing something every kid has done since the first crayons were invented. I refer to my car as the forty-thousand-dollar trash can, because it's full of Cheerios and Goldfish and leftover pb&j sandwiches. If I have to be in a car all the time, I can't always be saying, "Don't eat that" and "Don't touch that." Yes, I try to love my environments, but not at the cost of my relationships.

Home is your refuge and should be the place where all the stresses of the outside world melt away. My house in LA is the nicest house I've ever owned. It might not be for everyone, but it fits me. It's also the first place I've ever lived that doesn't have white walls. White walls. Who hasn't lived with white walls? White is so light and clean and practical. It matches everything. I thought it was "me" to have white walls. Who could argue with white? Well, I'm about to. I'm not against some white. But all-over white is another story. White isn't about matching everything. It's about being afraid of risk, experimentation, change.

Instead of accepting the image of myself that I'd always had, I decided to change the recipe in this house. I wanted to be more daring. I wondered what effect other colors might have on me. Paint is cheap, and a little goes a long way. If you buy a small can to see how painting your closet door banana yellow makes you feel, no harm done. You can always redo it. White is neutral. Harmless. Safe. But color is inspiring. It's emotional. It takes you places. And that's what your house should do. It should transport you to a place of peace and contentment. And so, what color did I paint my bedroom? Drumroll, please . . . purple. My bedroom is purple. Not Barney purple (that would *not* be okay), but an earthy, subtle purple that goes excellently with chocolate brown. And I'd be happy to never leave it. And that's not all. I have nutmeg red in my entrance hall. Red is a Big Commitment, a risky color. But I don't want to be safe. If it's wrong, or I start to hate it, I'll change it. But painting the walls makes them part of your home instead of the generic container in which all your stuff floats, unattached. It grounds you. It's an investment in your environment. It's warmer and more homey.

When it came to decorating my living room I found a swatch of fabric I thought was the happiest fabric I'd ever seen. I laughed out loud when I saw it. It's white, with a turquoise, pink, and gold pattern. It's casual, inviting, and whimsical. It felt like me. Not exactly like me—then it would have had a few rips and tears and ink spots of despair. More like my ideal for myself. But I had to face the cold, hard truth: It would make a horrible couch. Pink and turquoise? It's a little too much. So I used it on some pillows and picked up the colors around the room. That fabric still makes me happy every time I see it. What I'm saying is that no matter what anyone tells you, it isn't a bad thing to fall in love with a couple pillows and let them dictate everything else. Love is love, and I for one don't think it's easy to find.

For all the effort I've put into my nest, it's by no means perfect. Whose is? It's that old familiar theme: nature vs. man. In my case, it's yellow jackets vs. woman. Apparently I'm not the only one who sees my home as a nest. In the summer our backyard is full of yellow jackets. Zillions of them. You can barely see the lawn. The pretty yard, where I thought Emerson and I would have barbecues and spend hours of play, is unusable in the summer. People say you're not supposed to worry about bees—that if you don't bother them they won't bother you. But when I get a fear in my head, it's hard to get rid of it. I saw *Jaws* when I was twelve, and I've been terrified of sharks ever since, thank you very much, Mr. Spielberg. Sure, sharks do exist and can be a real threat. But do they hang out in lakes and the deep ends of pools? Unlikely. Also, in sixth grade there was one of those Mikey-ate-Pop-Rocks-drank-Coke-and-died urban legends floating around school about a plague of killer bees. A joke? A rumor? A plot by the sixth-grade boys to keep us off the lawn at recess? Whatever the origin, I've never stopped wondering—where are those mutant bees now? Are they the ones assembling forces for world domination in my backyard? No? How can you be so sure? I know. Irrational fears. There are so many of them, half real, half fiction—spiders, ants, the dangers of swimming after eating or sleeping on your stomach. I try my best not to pass the nutty ones on to Emerson.

I did try to get rid of the bees. No matter how many pest control people I hire to put hideous extermination tents out over the yard, no matter how many traps I buy, the yellow jackets win. I've admitted defeat. There's no way I can make my backyard a comfortable place to be in bee season. (Great. Now I've permanently lowered the resale value of my house. Not that I have plans to move. But to any prospective buyers out there, um, I'm sure there's a way to get rid of the bees. It's really only a couple days of the year. And they are a rare breed of extremely gentle, human-friendly yellow jackets who love to read literary fiction and sing show tunes on request, I swear.)

The bees conquered my backyard. But the fabricated, exaggerated, shark-level fears I try to subdue. It comes back to spending less time worrying about what might go wrong or planning for disaster. It's better to believe that life and people (and insects) are basically good and that we are strong enough to handle bad things when they come up, which they always do.

What is the value of material stuff? Thoreau said, "That man is the richest whose pleasures are the cheapest." I know nothing about wine. I mean, I know what I like when I taste it, but I've made absolutely no effort to educate myself so I can remember what I actually like. So what do I do? When I go to a restaurant and get stuck picking the wine, I look at how much the bottles cost. I figure the most expensive is the best, and the cheapest is the worst. I pick based on price. How lame is that? I know that some cheap wines are better than some expensive ones. Wine experts say that all the time. But when we're insecure that's what we do. We figure expensive must be better.

Take the painting above the fireplace in my den. I bought it at a garage sale for five dollars. It's a still-life of bottles and fruit, and it picks up the retro colors (rust, brown, turquoise, and gold) in my den. I love it. I've never asked anyone else what they thought about it, and not a single visitor has ever commented on it (which can't be a good sign). But that's not the point. It makes me happy. Or take the flint crystal glasses from the 1880s that I got in Nashville at an antique fair with Miss Gorgeous. They're more than glasses to me. They're so loaded with memories—the trip with my friend, being in Nashville, the fact that we got stuck there in a snowstorm which gave us time to go to an antique show, and the process of choosing and buying them. Every time I drink out of them, it's like I get to put on cowboy boots and a hat and dance a two-step, because that's what we did in Nashville. And then who cares if I know nothing about wine. All I know is it tastes good, which is enough for me.

Is it about how much something costs, or is it about the meaning of the object in your life? A little while ago I did a photo shoot for the cover of a magazine called *LA Confidential*. For those fashion shoots there are always a number of couture dresses for me to wear. Dior, Versace, Dolce & Gabbana. Fantastic dresses that cost at least $20,000 each. Often only one of these dresses exists in the entire world, and I get to wear it in a photo shoot. Now, I would never spend that much money on a dress. Oh my God no. Sure, I get that there are people who are unbelievably wealthy and for whom $20,000 is nothing. Yeah, there must be at least five people like that. But even so, you can only wear a unique couture dress once. Last time I did one of these shoots, I asked about the diamond necklace I was wearing for the shoot. "How much is this worth?" I asked. "A million dollars?" No, apparently it was a steal at $225,000. How much money do you have to have for that to be a necklace that you'd casually buy? The stylist said that there are people who'd spend half the money in their bank accounts on a necklace like that. It's a different way to be—to choose or need to spend most of your money on clothes and jewelry.

That relationship to dresses and jewelry fascinates me, not because I have any desire to be so . . . spendy. But the same way it was also hard for me to admit success and rent a limo, it was hard for me to acknowledge that success by making any changes in my lifestyle. Making it big (if playing Lois Lane on network television counts as making it big—maybe I should say making it *medium*) doesn't transform you overnight. It was and continues to be pretty hard for me to spend money. I still go to garage sales. Just the other day I bought a standing umbrella (for poolside shade) for seven dollars. I've always wanted one of those and they normally cost a hundred dollars new. So that made me happy. Little things do make me happy. I still clip coupons. I still love a sale. It's good to live frugally and responsibly. And it's hard to imagine anything making me happier than a good bowl of steamed clams, a sunset, a hug from my daughter, a black-and-white milk shake, a ride in a convertible, a warm bath, a massage, and a good pair of jeans and a t-shirt.

The arc of the first year of *Desperate Housewives* would take me from being interviewed by Diane Sawyer to being nominated for an Emmy. They have a party for all the nominees at Spago in Beverly Hills, Wolfgang Puck's super-Hollywood flagship restaurant. You'd think if there were one thing I'd be looking forward to it would be the celebration of that long-awaited recognition. But guess what? I forgot. That's right, I forgot about the whole thing. It was Friday, I was home with Emerson after school, getting ready for a night in with a book, ice cream, a fire, and a few games—Clue, Sorry!, and chess—lined up and ready for action. Then the phone rang. It was my friend asking, "So what time are you getting there?" I said, "Where?" Totally clueless. I guess it's no huge industry secret that we actresses borrow outfits for special events: dress, jewelry, shoes, and all, and return them like Cinderella the next morning. I had nothing to wear and no babysitter. So I asked Emerson if she'd be okay with sharing that kind of evening, promised her a lot of chocolate (Dove chocolate was the sponsor), and pulled out a vintage black '60s dress that I bought years ago at an English garage sale for eight dollars. I dressed it up with some new heels and diamond earrings, threw my hair into an updo, and we were off. I was just as happy in that dress as I'd have been in some carefully planned couture selection. Even happier, because I was proud of my well-spent eight bucks.

Just because I started making some money didn't mean my core values and needs changed. I don't know if they ever do. But there's something on the other side. It's important to be able to reward yourself. Of course it doesn't have to be with things, it can be with time to yourself. Or a trip. Or a party. Or a hike to a mountaintop. Everybody has to work on something. If you're like me, and spending money on yourself is hard to do, then rewarding yourself is one of those things worth working on.

When *Lois & Clark* was renewed for its second season, I forced myself to go to Barneys—which is not an inexpensive way to spend an afternoon—and bought myself several pieces of jewelry all at once. It felt so decadent. I nearly had a heart attack. I have no trouble taking friends out to dinner or buying presents for people, but I had never spent so much money on myself. Obviously we can't do that every day. That was a special moment, and it was ten years ago now, but I still wear and love those pieces. I wore one of the rings to the set of *Desperate Housewives* recently. It's a pretty ring—two thin gold bands with white gold flowers in between. One of the cast noticed the ring and complimented it, and there was an undertone in her voice suggesting that it might be from a new beau. I told her, in a half-deflated, half-proud voice, that I bought it for myself. The feeling that went with the ring ran deep, because it went back a long time, marking the years since my original purchase. It reminded me that I felt good enough about myself to have bought this ring. It reminded me that it's okay to feel beautiful and important sometimes. And it reminded me that for once I had bought something that didn't go out of style the next year. It's not shallow or overly self-indulgent to give yourself the present of something that makes you feel pretty and successful, and reminds you of that whenever you look at it. Hard as it may be to reward yourself, it's important to take the time and space to acknowledge achievement. Like renting that limo, which I should have done but never did. Or getting a massage on your birthday. And if you're going to indulge, don't just go through the motions. Make a big deal of it. Plan it in advance, let yourself get excited. Whether it's landing a new job, surviving last week, or sending your kid to kindergarten, tell yourself, *This is what I'm doing to celebrate.* Give it weight and permanence, and even if it isn't jewelry, it'll last a long time.

Of all the stuff we accumulate and value, jewelry tends to be the most meaningful (and the most prone to getting lost). I'm not obsessed with jewelry, but it's a perfect representation of the emotional attachment and symbolism that we afford material possessions. There's something magical about jewelry. When I went to London with Emerson all she cared about was going to the Tower of London. She was dying to see the Crown Jewels. In the gift shop we bought her a tiara, and I have to say that wearing it transformed my down-to-earth little girl into a princess. Jewels are more than mere adornments. They are and have been symbols throughout history. They represent love and family and status and religion and virtue. Every culture bejewels itself, from Native American turquoise, representing sky and water, to Chinese jade, believed to preserve the body after death. We're told in ads every day that jewelry represents love, desire, a promise.

There's a jewelry designer called Me&Ro that has some interesting jewelry with symbols and meaning. There was a piece with a skull on it that caught my eye. Recently my daughter has been really into black and skulls. Now most parents, including me, might find that a bit concerning. Why is my daughter into skulls? What does it mean? Is she obsessed with death? I started looking into the symbol of the skull and what it stands for.

It turns out that the skull is a reminder that everything will pass, and that in facing and embracing the reality of mortality, we find the strength to live fully and, more important, mindfully. I've always loved this concept of being mindful. I remember reading a book when I was pregnant about parenting mindfully. It sounds like a strange concept. But it's really simple and quite beautiful. Being mindful means being present, being conscious of your decisions and choices at all times. And being mindful gives you control of yourself and the situation. That control is calming to you and the people around you. So it all works in a positive spiral as opposed to the downward rabbit hole spiral I'm so prone to follow. Accepting the limitations of mortality reminds you of what is infinite—the choices and control that you have in life. We decorate ourselves with symbols and messages all the time, but none of it is meaningful until you stop to contemplate the resonance it has for you.

I've lost three necklaces—well, I've lost more than that, but each of these three meant something different to me. Each time something is lost, the experience is different. Emerson's best friend recently gave her a necklace with a dragonfly on it. She adored it, and the day after she got it she wore it over to my friend Cris's house. We had a full day. There was dress up and picture-drawing and fort-making, and somewhere along the way, Emerson lost the necklace. We all looked everywhere for it, but it was nowhere to be found in Cris's big house. It was gone. Emerson was upset, and part of me wanted to just end her pain. I knew where to buy the necklace, and it wasn't expensive. But if a kid loses or destroys something, you can't always just say, "It's okay. I'll buy you another one." Emerson's almost eight, and she's ready to take some responsibility for her belongings. So I told her I was sorry she was sad, and that I'd give her plenty of hugs if they made her feel better, but that was it. I reminded her that maybe next time she took off a necklace she cared about, she'd remember to put it in a specific place. This is hard parenting, and you don't have to do it every time. But you also need to teach kids to keep track of their stuff.

What Emerson didn't know (but I'll tell her one day when she's old enough or if she reads this book, which she'd better not because I don't know how I'm going to explain that story about the massage) is that I once lost a pair of necklaces that she gave me. When she was about five years old, she really wanted to get me a Mother's Day present, but she wanted it to be a surprise. So my girlfriend and I set it up that the three of us went into a store. I wandered around saying pointedly, "This is a nice scarf" and "Oh, I like this shirt" and "Wow, those are really nice necklaces." Then my friend asked me to go get some coffee for the grown-ups, and while I was gone Emerson "secretly" decided to get me a pretty set of two necklaces—one had a big "O" on it, and one had a little "o." Like mother and daughter necklaces. She was so proud of pulling off her little scheme and loved to see me wear the necklaces. But a few months later, I couldn't find them. I was horrified. And that time I went back and bought them again. Not because I wasn't willing to suffer the consequences of my own irresponsibility, but because I didn't want her to know I'd lost the gift that meant so much.

I'm not a hypocrite—I don't always replace my own necklaces. I know when and how to bear the burden of loss. As I've mentioned, my mother's not much of a shopper. She got her first pedicure at age sixty-nine. When I was a kid, she'd take me to buy my back-to-school clothes, but I always had a fantasy that we'd shop together the way mothers and daughters do. Just for fun, stopping for lunch or a Shirley Temple, being girly together. I still kind of have that fantasy, so about seven years ago I took her to lunch in Beverly Hills and shopping at Fred Segal. We had a really nice day. In the jewelry department, I saw a necklace that I thought was sweet. It was a black beaded choker with a charm that said "spirit." My mother asked if she could buy it for me. I said yes—I liked the idea that she was giving me spirit. But I managed to lose that necklace too. (I'm sure it's here somewhere!) I was sad about it, but that one I didn't replace. Because I knew that the important thing was having that experience with my mother. The necklace had done its job, and another one could never replace it.

Stuff has its merits. It's an experience, a reward, an opportunity to reassess what's important in life, but at some point every new thing you buy becomes just one more thing you have to dust. And if you live in California like I do, you know it's all gonna break in the earthquake anyway. And your closet's too small. Owning things is stressful and, for the most part, unnecessary. Emerson, as always, said it best. Last time we went camping, we packed up our shabby Scooby-Doo van and climbed in. I love camping with her, and I live in fear of the day when she's a teenager and would rather practice using a curling iron with her friends than camp with me. But for now, we both have nothing we'd rather do. For all the value and experience and memories that come from our possessions, it all takes a backseat to the majestic seascapes of the Pacific Coast Highway. As we headed north in our slow and not-so-steady wagon, Emerson turned to me and said, "We could live in here, Mommy. This is all we need." Amen to that.

It's Pretty, Let's Eat It

I grew up fishing. The first time I caught, killed, and cleaned a fish all by myself was when I was eleven. I had wandered off from our campsite in Sonoma into the hills on a barely existing trail and spotted a small eddy (where the water circles back out of the rapids in the opposite direction, creating a calm spot) that looked like a good place for fish to rest after the turmoil of the rough stream. I settled on a flat rock and put a wriggling worm on the hook. (I always feel conflicted about that heartless worm-hooking. I like being the girl who's not afraid to dig in the dirt, handle a worm, and put it on a hook. But I don't like killing anything either, so to give it that stab through its middle then basically let it drown while waiting to be eaten—it leaves me feeling, shall we say, guilty.) Anyway, after a long interlude of bird-watching and wondering if a bear might be around, I felt that first tug. I was so exhilarated. I always wanted to make my dad proud, and I knew this would do it. Jerking back at just the right time, I hooked the mouth and reeled him in. He was a big trout, and I didn't have a net, so I carefully dragged him up the shore making sure not to break the line.

Then I found a small rock, bonked him on the head to put him out of his misery, and triumphantly carried him back to my dad. Later we ate him for dinner. (Camping fish tip: Place sliced lemon, salt, pepper, and olive oil on fish and wrap in foil. Cook over fire. Yum. Delicious.) He was fourteen inches long—and I swear he hasn't grown an inch in thirty years of boasting!

I took Emerson fishing for the first time when she was four and a half. My dad sweetly bought her a fishing pole. It was a kids' pole—purple and plastic. Not the strongest pole in the world, but a short, easy-to-use pole with a real hook and line. It wasn't meant for anything tricky like fly-fishing or trolling. You could cast out about fifteen feet, then sit and wait to see if a fish bit. We took Emerson's new pole with us, went into the mountains, and found a nice campsite by a lake. I put salmon eggs on the hook for her (I thought I'd spare her the whole torture-the-worm thing seeing as we were about to possibly kill a fish), and she cast it in all by herself. We let it sink, and then I propped the pole between some rocks so it was sitting up by itself. I didn't really expect her to catch anything. We were just going to relax and enjoy ourselves, and if we saw a tug at the line, she could try to reel it in.

We spread out a blanket and I started to read her *Anne of Green Gables*. Before I was a minute into the book the pole jerked down. I jumped up. "Honey, you got a bite!" Emerson ran over and started reeling it in. It was a trout all right, just like my first catch (only smaller, but who's counting?). It was definitely a respectable, edible, beautiful rainbow trout, glistening in the sun just beneath the water as she reeled it in. They don't call it rainbow trout for nothing. She looked at its gleaming silver, pink, and green scales and said, "Oh Mom, it's so pretty!" And this was it, this was the moment I imagined might happen, that it would just be too hard and confusing and complicated to kill a beautiful fish. I knelt down, slipped an arm around her, and said,

"It *is* really pretty, do you want to throw it back?" and with a gleam in her eye, she looked up at me and said, "No, let's eat it!" and with a smile I thought, *Yep, that's my daughter.*

Being a celebrity in Hollywood is a little like being that poor fish. They tell you you're pretty, then they eat you up. One day, they air-brush your image for a magazine cover and all you hear is how gorgeous you are; the next they snap your picture while you're taking out the garbage in your pajamas, and print it with the headline "Stars without Their Makeup." I know the whole tabloid-paparazzi-in-your-front-yard thing isn't something we all face on a daily basis. But it's one example of how society treats women. It reinforces unrealistic expectations about our appearances, and that constant judgment has an effect on us and even our daughters.

Much as I have trouble believing I'm forty sometimes (don't we all feel twenty-eight in our heads forever?), the fact is that I am. I know I've been fortunate to maintain my looks—I guess being cast on *Desperate Housewives* is affirmation of that. But that doesn't mean my whole body doesn't feel its age. I call it the Bounce Back Factor. When I was twenty I could have a few drinks, cry over the latest rejection, get a few hours sleep, and be fresh and perky the next day. Now, if I cry, if I don't sleep much, if I don't support my body with water and good, healthy food, well, let's just say, my makeup artist really has his work cut out for him. Sometimes in my business I can find myself working fifteen hours a day several days in a row. While even ten years ago I could keep that up for weeks, now at that pace I feel like I've been hit by a truck when it's over. Nevertheless, it's true that forty has been an amazing year for me. I got my first beauty campaigns with Clairol and Hydroderm. I'm part of a hit TV show and have been fortunate enough to grace some important magazine covers, getting to work with great photographers, makeup artists, hairdressers, and stylists. So you might understand my surprise when a magazine emailed me cheerily informing me that they were going to print my photo alongside the opinions of a panel of plastic surgeons making recommendations as to the kind of "work" I needed. They do this to some lucky woman each month. Lovely.

Here's something you need to know. Most actors have publicists. I had one during the *Lois & Clark* days—in fact he's still a good friend of mine—but during the . . . what should we call it? During my "kitchen floor phase" I didn't need one. Then, when *Desperate Housewives* started, I just decided I didn't want one. So I, along with maybe three other actresses in Hollywood, don't have a publicist. I like dealing with people directly and I think anytime you can eliminate the layers of people who relay messages, you get a clearer, more accurate communication of what's actually happening. Also, part of my whole forty-year-old revelation is that I want to believe I can trust people. Trust is an area I need work on, so giving over to the idea that I don't constantly have to be protecting myself from everyone seemed like a good fit for me. No one is out there "creating my image," if that can even truly be done. It's just me, living my life, answering lots of requests, setting up talk-show appearances, magazine shoots, and charity events.

So I emailed the tabloid back. I was horrified at the idea that some plastic surgeons who'd never met me and knew nothing of my medical history or my current health would make suggestions about how, under general anesthetic, I could have cosmetic manipulations to improve my face and body. I wrote, "Wow. First of all, I am so sorry for your readers. I cannot believe that this is what you want to put out there for women. What kind of message do you think you are sending to women, when you tell them that a celebrity—Teri Hatcher, a woman who has had a second chance, who has had a great year, has a great job, won awards, made money, and has a beautiful daughter— that even *she* needs plastic surgery to be 'better'?" What is better? To what end was this suggested surgery supposed to help me? If I got a face-lift, would I be happier? Would I be on a better TV show? Would I make more money? Oh I know! I would probably be able to get a boyfriend, yeah, that's my problem. Jeez, thanks for that suggestion. It was infuriating to me that this is what they wanted to perpetuate. It's sick.

I had a guest appearance on a *Seinfeld* episode before Emerson was born, throughout which Jerry and Elaine debated whether my breasts were real. My parting line, which got the kind of attention that so much of the great writing on *Seinfeld* garnered, was, "They're real, and they're spectacular." Well, they're still real, but now they're more spectacular in a bra, especially if the bra is made by La Perla. I can't overstate the importance of a good bra. I mean, my breasts are just fine, but they're not twenty. I remember when I was a girl hearing that if you could stick a pencil under your breast and it stayed then you needed to wear a bra. Well, I need one.

The world tells us we need to look a certain way, but therapists tell us we need to accept ourselves the way we are. We need to love our natural bodies. At least I think that's what therapists say. I don't have a therapist, but if I did and she was any good, I'm sure that's what she'd be saying. She'd remind me that women get older, skin sags, wrinkles appear, and the wisdom of accepting that is part of an aging woman's beauty. We ladies get a lot of conflicting messages about body and health from the media. I, for one, am cheering for the "love your body the way it is" side. Every mother knows what happens after you've breast-fed. It's like those precious, adorable, ravenous babies suck the tissue right out of you. I remember feeling like I was actually losing bone mass. I like my body, I do. I like it more when it's strong, when I can see little arm muscles and feel the soreness in my thighs after riding a horse. But no workout routine is going to bring back my boobs. And I know it.

I haven't had a boob job. I've thought about it, but I just can't bring myself to go there. I'd rather use the adhesive body bra by Fashion Forms. They call it "the liberating alternative to a strapless bra." I call it the removable boob job. And if that doesn't work, I'll use gaffer's tape. That's right, gaffer's tape. Another perfect temporary boob job, that gummy silver duct tape that most people use on cars or wires or to hold together torn vinyl seats (like the ones in my VW van). This is a secret I really want you to have. When you wear those complicated, low-cut dresses, and you're forty, that's how you can achieve perfect cleavage. Any model or Hollywood actress who wears fancy designer ball gowns knows how to expertly manipulate gaffer's tape to mush, lift, and hold your breasts like a bra. Sexy, huh? Now imagine slinking out of a gown to reveal that to a new lover. Hey baby, check out my taped-up boobs. So silvery, so sleek. So not happening. You definitely have to slip into the ladies room and pull that tape off before anyone tries to get to third base. I'm telling you, it's very glamorous. NOT.

I know I keep joking about my boobs, but you won't hear one complaint about my nipples. They're awesome. Okay, so here's the thing. My editor asked me if I really wanted to talk about my nipples. Fair enough. Who wants to hear about anyone else's nipples? (For that matter, why do I talk so much about my boobs? I joke about them on talk shows and in articles, I guess because they're the definitive feminine symbol, and there ought to be a way for them to be real and spectacular at forty—because they're you and you're them.) But I gave the nipple quandary some thought and decided I *do* want to talk about them. Here's the deal: We all have parts of our bodies that we love effortlessly, that we don't think about or try to change. Then there are the parts that we always think about and try to change. So I happen to be happy with my nipples. That doesn't mean they're big or small or objectively that great, but they are to me. (I have an awesome little negligee that actually has a small slit in the nipple area. It came from the store that way, so I'm thinking if a clothing company is designing sleepwear with such easy nipple access, then I must not be the only person who feels good about her nipples.) If I can find one feature that

I feel good about, admit it, and put it in a book, then maybe it will help you find some part of you that you can really appreciate. Feeling that way about your body is an end in itself. And—bonus—it's surely the first step to finding someone who loves you, loves all of you, and treasures your body and doesn't have to look past it or cover it with state-of-the-art underwire. That's who I'm looking for—applications now being accepted.

But let me clarify: I don't judge people who have work done to feel better about their bodies. I have girlfriends, all different looking. Some have careers, some are moms, some are both. The one thing we all have in common is that we want the day to come that we feel good about ourselves. We all want what we don't have. If our hair's curly, we want it straight. If we're flat-chested, we want big boobs (preferably not saggy ones). If we're narrow-hipped, we want a womanly figure. And vice versa. It's hard to accept what we were given. The grass is always greener. When and if you actually get to the other side of the fence, it doesn't necessarily get easier to accept your own unique beauty. In fact, you're probably exhausted and covered with splinters by then.

Some of my friends have found that after lots of different cuttings and liftings—and agonizing recoveries—they felt happier. But some of them have not. They still ask themselves when and how they will get to the day when they finally feel good about themselves. I ask myself the same question. How did I get this way? How did I learn to *not* like myself in the first place? Our mothers get blamed for a lot of this stuff, and though I hate to say it, it's true that mom is our first role model. Moms can be hard on us because they love us so much. They really do want the best for us and they think their critical eye might help us avoid later disasters. Sometimes I think if my mother had felt better about herself as I was growing up, I would have had the permission to feel good about myself. That may be why I was always begging her to wear a dress or put on perfume or mascara. (I think I was the first one to buy her Chanel No. 5, which is still her favorite.) But the bottom line is, it doesn't really matter how you got to feeling this way about yourself. Now is the time to take responsibility for your body. Own it and love it and if you don't, make constructive changes that will lead you down that path.

How I feel about myself is directly tied to how I treat myself. There was a period when I was about twenty when I was so depressed that all I would do was stay in my small apartment, eat fried chicken delivered from Popeyes, and walk a block to the corner grocer for a pint of Häagen-Dazs ice cream (chocolate chocolate chip) every day. I did gain a few pounds and, actually, as I recall, it was the first time I ever thought about dieting.

At the time I was playing a mermaid on *The Love Boat*. I wasn't the best of the eight dancers, but apparently I had some glimmer, some humor, some something that got me noticed anyway. Our choreographer told me that I was gaining a little weight. I wasn't any normal American's idea of overweight, but in that realm of dancers, where weight issues are much worse than with actresses, I guess it was noticeable, especially in my tummy. So I started exercising. I started jogging. I remember wanting to "be in better shape" so badly that on my lunch hour I'd jog around Hollywood in the 102-degree heat in a stage-two smog alert. I'm sure *that* was healthy. I joined the first of many gyms I would go to. I hired the first of many trainers I would use (one of whom I married, briefly). And I always hated it. For the first time in my life, being active felt like something I had to do.

When I was a kid I took a lot of dance classes. I danced 'cause it was fun and it made me feel special. Not everyone could do it. Not everyone had the discipline. I knew I wasn't the best of the dancers, but I held my own and it gave me an identity. I didn't take jazz and ballet for exercise. Hell, I didn't even use that word. Exercise is a word that adults use to describe the activity they don't enjoy but feel guilted into doing. As an adult, activity became an obligation, starting with the jogging, and increasing as I dealt with the hours I worked on *Lois & Clark*, and, eventually, the challenges of mothering. Skiing was a sport I grew up loving so much that I would get up at 4 A.M. to drive the three hours to Alpine up by Lake Tahoe, ski all day, and drive back. But even skiing became a chore. I preferred to spend my winter holidays in the lodge with a scotch.

So I realize that to many who struggle with weight, it seems like I should feel lucky that I've never really had to diet. And I do. But as I mentioned before, the grass on the other side of the fence can have weeds in it too. Skinny teenagers aren't cool either. I was teased with the nickname "Spider Legs" my whole life. And as desperate as I was to look cute in my Calvins, they just didn't cut it on my flat ass. I was also teased with "Hairy Teri"—watch the tabloids eat that up—but I won the hair battle with tweezers and wax. I watched my mother try to lose twenty pounds for *thirty years*. I still watch her and other people I love torture and deny themselves in an attempt to change numbers on a scale. I myself struggle not to use food as an emotional replacement for things that are missing in my life. So it's no surprise that I've ended up looking in the refrigerator for a guy. He's never in there. Only food. And some of it expired. I'll search the cupboards for something to take his place: macaroni and cheese, chips, cookies. (It's always the same combo with comfort food . . . hot starch, salt, and sugary fat. Is that what men are made of? Hmmm.)

Anyway, when I recognize and admit these generational issues I'm carrying on, it makes it all the more important to me to stop the madness for Emerson's sake. I finally found some kind of working out (notice what I didn't call it?) that I enjoy and I let her see that. In my bedroom I keep a few dumbbells and a mat. I do push-ups, sit-ups, bicep curls, squats, and other isometrics. Sometimes Emerson and I play games like charades while I lift weights. Or we talk or she colors. She's so happily oblivious to "exercise" that she's started rotating through the elliptical trainer and the weights with me. She thinks it's fun. And, you know what? It is. We found that we both love horseback riding, another form of beneficial fun that she calls playing and I call the right way to stick with exercising.

I'm also conscious of helping Emerson know she can trust herself with food. I don't know how many of you have had sleepover play-dates. It seems like there are two kinds of kids—the type who want to sleep over at others' houses and the type who want to host the sleep-over at home. My daughter is the latter. We've been hosting sleepovers since she was five. In fact, we are having one tonight. (So now you can picture me writing on my computer. It's Saturday morning. I'm in my pj's with a cup of coffee, knowing that in eight hours, four little girls will be running around, screaming with delight, making homemade ice cream, and leaving trails of toys as they move from one game to the next. There's going to be a lot of coffee drunk by this mommy before this day is through.)

The morning after one particular sleepover, I was downstairs making pancakes and fruit for Emerson and her friend, and they were playing upstairs. I went up to let them know that breakfast was ready. When I opened the door, I found them huddled amidst some dress-up clothes already eating their first meal of the day. However, today their version of breakfast was M&M's. I said, "What are you girls doing?" The other little girl got very shy, huddling so deep into the princess outfits that all I could see of her was through lace and frills. My daughter said, "We're having M&M's for breakfast." I said, "Oh, okay, well, I've got pancakes downstairs when you're ready."

As I turned to walk down the hall, I stopped and thought about the expression I'd seen on Emerson's friend's face. It was painful to see a child feel such shame about what she was doing. I saw the beginning, the seven-year-old beginning, of eating issues. Without any purposeful harm from her parents—which I know for sure because they happen to be some of my best friends—this little girl I love was feeling guilty, and it was about her relationship with food. Now some parents choose to keep things like candy away from their kids so they can't eat it all the time. That's one choice. Another is to put all the snack stuff on a reachable shelf from an early age so that the child learns that she can make choices about when to snack based on her hunger needs. I take it a step further. Emerson is actually allowed to keep a box of candy in her room. It usually sits on a shelf in her closet and contains some left-over Easter, Halloween, and generally accumulated goodies from different events. I let her have it there because I trust her. The result is that she doesn't associate food with reward or punishment. She's become very responsible about her eating choices. She's a good eater; she eats when she's hungry, not more or less; she eats a variety of food; she likes trying new things; and she helps prepare meals with me.

In the hallway I realized I might have a small opportunity to let this friend of hers see food a little differently, while clearly reinforcing my boundaries and expectations for Emerson. I opened the door again. They both froze like deer in headlights. I said with a calm smile, "Emerson, I just wanted you to know that I trust you with food. That's why I let you have the candy in your room—because I believe you know when you've had enough candy and you know what is right for your body and what is not. If you want to have M&M's for breakfast once in a while, like on a special sleepover date, well, I think that's fine." Without waiting for a response, I gently closed the door and hoped all that landed. I hoped a feeling of acceptance, not punishment, would wrap around them both for those few little minutes and they would feel good about themselves.

Ideally, the focus of eating should be health consciousness mixed with the joy of food. Thin is not inherently healthy and fat is not inherently unhealthy. Health is determined by your cholesterol, blood pressure, EKGs, blood tests, lung power, and so on. Just because I'm thin doesn't mean I can get away with eating comfort food. Those same genes that give me the high metabolism to keep me thin also saddle me with high cholesterol. Mine has shot up as high as 275. I saw a nutritionist not to lose weight but to lower my cholesterol. Not to be thin but to be healthy. Not to take away from my body but to give it the right things. Not to diet! Dieting is such a big part of so many people's daily routines, and it affects your ability to enjoy your life. That's my beef with it and that's why I'm weighing in. In fact, I hate the word "diet." I hate the word "hate" too. But hating the word "diet" seems like exactly the right description of my feelings, so I'll forgo my ban on the word "hate," just this once. I hate it for what it's done to my mother and my friends and all the women who struggle with food. I'm all for declaring a National Throw Out the Scales Day. Doesn't that sound like an idea Oprah would have? Once I heard her say that you only have to decide to do something and you can do it. That made sense to me since I feel like I've spent a lot of my first year in my forties deciding to be happy, deciding to be successful, deciding to not eat the burnt toast.

There is no right weight. There's only good health. What's healthy for you. If you want to eat healthily but don't, ask yourself what's standing in your way. Are you afraid of being the absolute best you can be, because (as Liz Phair says) "if you do it and you're still unhappy, then you know that the problem is you"? Are you afraid of having no excuses for your unhappiness, nothing to blame it on? If you were at your best, would your husband feel threatened? Would you have to have sex with your partner and admit to problems there? Would you have to take responsibility for things you don't want to deal with? Are you uncomfortable being a winner? I can ask you all these questions because I've asked them of myself. They're questions I turn to when I look at my good life and wonder why I still have trouble liking myself.

Only you know why you hold on to weight and bad eating habits. I have a memory of my mother (and it's not that hard to recall because she still does it forty years later) that after a meal, especially a fine meal at a restaurant, she would say "Moo." I'm not kidding. Moooo. I came to hate that put-down of herself. In fact it makes me cringe just to write it. But it's the truth. My mother mooed after most meals, and I learned to associate guilt with pleasure. Right after I did something I enjoyed, I'd put myself down. I learned to stop my fun in its tracks. You see, my mother's behavior translated into something much bigger than food. It was the whole notion of joy that she was condemning with her bovine articulation.

Only you can figure out why you devalue yourself. I figured out that I've been afraid to be strong, confident, funny, smart, and beautiful. My fear is that if I let myself be all that and life still doesn't go well—then what? When I turned forty I made a conscious decision to live the next decade of my life as a good winner instead of a protected loser, and I've been lucky to have such instant karmic feedback. I decided to be different. And though I don't succeed at it every day, though that old burnt toast voice whispers its way back into my brain, sometimes saying "Moooo," I hear it less often and filter it out more quickly. I try to focus on the decision to be healthy. Decide to reach your goal, and then do it.

The real goals of our lives are happiness, health, comfort, femininity, and so on. Thin isn't really a goal. We just get convinced that it's the *means* to the end. Well, I'm here to say it isn't. I sit at home alone many a night with my "enviably" skinny legs while plenty of bigger women are out having the time of their lives. Skinny isn't making me happier, or healthier. It's not making me live longer. If you want to be happier, you have to shift your perception of yourself, of other people, of the world. And you have to plan.

Planning takes time, time you must allow yourself to take 'cause you deserve it. When I make my plans for the day or the week, I include meals. Don't let food be an afterthought. In fact don't let *yourself* be an afterthought. Sometimes I put myself so last that even the goldfish get fed before me. I'm not kidding. Everyone will be taken care of and I'll be pinching fish food into the bowl when I realize that I haven't eaten, let alone showered. When you include meals in your day, you won't let that hunger make you reach for fast junk like a handful of Goldfish (the snack food, not the pet!) or a bag of potato chips. Eating like that doesn't nourish you. You (in theory) plan your schedule, your finances, your household. Plan your nutritional life, too.

I love to empty my pantry and refrigerator and start again. Emerson and I do this together, and it's a good way to stay in touch with what your household really eats. Refill it with things you want to eat. Not just fat-free stuff (honestly, I hate that crap). Think about your lifestyle. I often find myself with little time or energy to cook. One thing I like is fresh sliced deli meat and organic cheese. I roll it up in iceberg lettuce like a taco. It's a quick, yummy protein-and-calcium snack that leaves me energized. Or stock raw almonds or walnuts. They're good for you, and they keep well in the glove compartment of the car (someone please tell me why it's still called a glove compartment?).

You know a lot of parents use the "if . . . then" bargain: "*If* you finish your dinner, *then* you can have dessert," or "*If* you stay in your car seat and stop screaming, *then* you can have this pack of Oreos." But my mother didn't really give me the "if . . . then" treatment, she sort of gave it to herself. She'd deny, deny, deny herself, then reward herself with a candy bar or a vanilla ice cream with chocolate sauce from Baskin-Robbins. Consequently, I'm no stranger to the pull toward the food reward system. Like I told you before, I try to keep it out of Emerson's life, and I try to keep it out of mine. But I can also relate to how, once you've blown it for the day with the fried chicken and ice cream, you might as well finish off the Cheetos and Mallomars. I've done that and still do it, though not often. So I've stopped bartering with myself. When I feel the pull to do it I stop and ask myself, "Why? Why am I doing damage to myself by eating too much? What am I sad about? Am I angry? Am I hiding away?" And so sometimes I'll just make myself reward myself for absolutely nothing. I'll go buy a new lotion or flowers for the nightstand, and each time I look at them I remember I deserve them for doing absolutely nothing except for being me.

This is the beginning of taking care of you. Choosing, deciding to treat yourself better. You can give yourself black licorice and gummy bears (two of my favorites) because you trust yourself with food and won't overindulge. You can buy yourself cute workout clothes before you lose weight. You can send yourself flowers because no one else is doing it right now. Liking yourself means wanting to put healthy things in your body: protein, carbs (yes, carbs), calcium, vegetables, etc. You know the drill. But you have to be careful because the food threshold is right there all the time. It's so easy to cross from pleasure to guilt, from nutrition to filling an emotional hole. So slow down. Take control of your experience. Make the effort to create a meal that is a healthy, positive experience. The guilt goes away, and that's just the beginning. Next thing you know, some authentic happiness will start to filter in. And that happiness will let you be a little less hard on yourself. You'll be able to start to like something about yourself, and if you have to start with your nipples, well, then there you go—someone did it before you, so it's okay. Maybe it's your eyes, or your hands, or the way you treat people, or your sense of humor. Whatever it is, find it, notice it, and watch it blossom.

It's ironic that I ended up in a business where looks matter so much when it's always been hard for me to feel comfortable in my own skin. Why do people gravitate toward acting? People say it's because we want applause or approval. We're seeking out attention and validation, but at the same time we're putting ourselves in a position where we're judged—and a lot of that judgment starts with the outside.

At some point there might be pressure on me to go under the knife. I'm regularly photographed, even in my private life. When the paparazzi take pictures of you in your bathing suit, you can't throw the bad ones in the garbage the way you might at home. More critically, one's appearance is such a big part of being an actress that it's possible at some point I'll start to hear that plastic surgery would help me get jobs. Can you imagine if a law firm or a science expedition told its female partners they needed to have a little work done? Can you scream sexual harassment? I know, I know. It's part of the business I happen to work in. Dear Lord. I sure hope that by the time I feel like I need to get plastic surgery to get a job in Hollywood I have enough money to quit the business. I'd certainly rather segue into other projects as I age. Maybe I'll open a roadside café in Montana. Produce projects for younger, sellable, non-saggy-boobed actresses and use my brain instead of my chest. Should I grow a business or have my body cut open for a paycheck? Hmmm. Use my brain or traumatize my body? Doesn't seem like a tough choice to me.

That choice isn't exactly on your radar when you're deciding to be an actor. When I took the job on *The Love Boat*, I didn't say to myself, "Well, here I go. People are going to spend so much time judging me on the outside, that everyone will forget there's a person behind all that hair and makeup." (Though the hair was so big in the '80s that I might have made an educated guess.) In fact, what I did think was that I'd temporarily move to LA, make more money per week than my mom made per month after twenty-five years at Lockheed, and then go back to college to finish my math degree, marry my high school boyfriend, and raise children in my hometown. Wow—that so did not happen. What did happen is I broke up with that boyfriend. He married my best friend. They sold a story about me to a tabloid for ten thousand dollars. I went out with a bartender, a dancer, then a trainer. I married the trainer. I divorced him eight months later. I thought about moving back home. I didn't. I got some parts in movies and TV. I dated an asshole who cheated on me with all of Paris. I split up with the asshole. I thought about moving home. I became the third Lois Lane. I got married. I had a baby. I got divorced. I thought about going home. I struggled with a lot. I got *Desperate Housewives*. And someone asked me to write a book. There. That's the tell-all part. Thank God I fit that in somewhere, you know, in case that's what people were expecting!

So here I am, twenty years later, emailing a tabloid to rant and rave about women and body image. They never emailed me back (that nutty Teri Hatcher sending midnight emails again), but they didn't run the article about how my face could be fixed by the miracles of modern science either. Success? Not exactly. They ran the very same article, but with a photo of Sarah Jessica Parker instead. But I wasn't just trying to kill an article about me. I was making a point about what they are doing to the women of this country! What are they saying— that successful, beautiful, healthy actresses need to make themselves better by having Botox injections and eyelifts? It's a sad state of affairs. I hope someday the magazines will listen, for their own sake, or for the sake of their wives, their daughters, or their future selves. Or, barring that, for the extreme heat they are going to feel in hell if they don't.

I think about how those magazines pretend to build a connection between celebrities and noncelebrities. Celebrities go shopping just like us! They stroll their babies just like us! They throw telephones at hotel clerks just like us! (Okay, they're all not *exactly* like us.) Last weekend Emerson and I were driving over Malibu Canyon to meet some friends. One-third of the way over the canyon I noticed that the gas gauge was below empty. The light was on. Gasp. We had no gas. Does anyone else do that—drive the car until the light starts flashing— actually past the flashing? I'm guilty of doing that more than once, as if the car will just run forever. Seems like with all the fancy computers in cars these days they should at least be programmed to be a little more articulate about exactly what that little light means. Would it kill them to put in the manual, "When the light goes on, you have approximately twenty miles of gas left. When the light flashes, you have twenty feet."? (Like I'd read the manual.) Anyway . . . I knew there was no gas station between us and the Pacific Coast Highway, and I didn't think we'd make it, so I pulled over to make a U-turn. As I pulled off the road, I saw in the rearview mirror a car doing the same thing. It was definitely not a normal place to turn. I was being followed.

It's creepy to realize that you're being followed, even when you know that it's the paparazzi. Women grow up feeling on guard and in danger when they're followed, and that feeling never goes away. You don't get used to it. Your instinct is to lose them, and I've tried that. They run lights to keep hounding you. It's not safe. Even though they are supposedly armed with only a camera, it feels, well . . . invasive! And even scary! And it's worse when it's not just you going through this, but your daughter too. So there I was, on the side of the highway, trying to make my turn. There was a ton of traffic, and I had to wait forever for a break in the cars. I wasn't trying to lose the guy, but I slipped into the stream of cars kind of hoping he'd just disappear. No such luck. By the time we finally pulled into a gas station, there were five cars following me. Three SUVs, a Honda, and an Excursion. All non-license-plated cars (God knows how they get away with that). I grabbed my sunglasses and a baseball cap from my beach bag (which I was fortunate to have since I was headed for the beach) and got out to pump the gas. They snapped pictures. I got back in the car while the gas was filling up, all the while trying not to let Emerson know. She's only seven, but it doesn't feel good to her either.

I know this kind of attention is part of the gig. I call it swallowing the celebrity bullet. But the part I hate most is how Emerson's private world is violated. She didn't choose my job, and she deserves to have a normal childhood. We could hide away and never go anywhere so we wouldn't be photographed, but that wouldn't be normal either. Whenever someone comes up to us during our personal time, I'm acutely aware that if I choose to take that picture or sign that autograph, I'm saying to my daughter, "You need to hang on for a second while I deal with this total stranger." It's hard. I'm grateful to my fans. I like to be accessible. I don't want to be curt and dismissive. I get it. Still, as it's gone on and on I see what it's doing to her. I realize what I'm communicating to her when I ask her to wait. In that moment, I become more important than her. Our balance is upset, and I don't blame her for not liking it. To her I'm just Mommy, and frankly, through it all, that's still how I'm most comfortable identifying myself. But what am I supposed to do? The answer isn't in the parenting books. Try looking in the index of any parenting book below "pacifier" and I guarantee you won't find "paparazzi." It's not in there. I work hard to make her feel important and to explain it to her. We talk about the good parts of fame—being invited as special guests to Disneyland, being able to afford an exotic trip. She tries to understand, but she's only seven. It's worth noting that while these tabloids are trying to show how we're just like everyone else, they're interfering with Emerson's right to have a normal childhood—to be like everyone else. And yes, I took this job. I bear the ultimate responsibility. That's exactly why I work so hard to protect her.

The tank was now full, and I hopped out of the car. I was nervous just knowing they were watching my every move—don't sneeze, don't pick your nose, make sure your sweats aren't in your butt crack, and oh God I'm wearing flip-flops and my toes aren't pedicured. (They've already done a ton of articles about my ugly feet. Can you imagine? They shoot close-ups of my feet! For the record, I like my toes just fine. Not as much as my nipples, but they're still suck-worthy. Applications accepted—oh, did I say that already?) Then, for the first time in all the zillions of times I've pumped gas, I pulled the nozzle out and the gas sprayed everywhere. From fifteen feet away, the cameras went wild. They got their money shot. When I got back in the car, I made light of it with Emerson, who by then had noticed that we had company. We knew the picture would be in the tabloids the next week. The only question was whether the headline would be "Fame hasn't gone to her head. Teri Hatcher still pumps her own gas," or, "Teri Hatcher is such a diva she can't even pump her own gas." I said to Emerson, "Let's make a bet. Is it going to be good or bad?" Emerson took "good." That left me with "bad," appropriately enough since I'm the more jaded one. (We were both right. Two different tabloids ran the same photo with exact opposite captions.)

What you see in the tabloids is not what you and I have in common. Buying coffee. Pumping gas. Who cares about that stuff? It has nothing to do with who you are. The real story of what we have in common is emotional, truthful, and human. It's how we try to live, and love, and find happiness, and work toward finding peace in ourselves and in the world. This is where we connect—not by what we seem to be doing on the outside, but how we feel on the inside.

Imagine you are jogging on a trail. It's a cool morning, and the sky is still blanketed with clouds. As you head up the hill you feel good. You feel strong. You didn't bring headphones because you thought it would be good to hear the sounds of nature: birds, dogs, squirrels, rattlesnakes. (Yes, rattlesnakes. I've more than once seen them sunning themselves right in the middle of the path. It's not a bad idea to have open eyes and ears for summer snake-time hikes in the mountains. If I were bitten I know I'd be photographed, but would I be rescued?)

So there you are, just starting to break a sweat, when you come upon two women who are walking slowly in the same direction you're headed. One of the women is sobbing, really sobbing, and the other is saying, "Well, men just do asshole things like that. They all do." You slow down, thinking, I don't want to pass them. It's too intimate and I can't interrupt. It won't go on forever. But the crier continues to wail about how awful it is and he is, and you realize that your jog is so slow that it's practically jumping jacks, so you speed up and run past. And if you're anything like me (which I hope you are in some small way because that's kind of the point of this book), you zoom out of earshot.

As I ran I started to think about what they were saying, about what it's like to have a marriage fall apart at middle age, and to have kids you love with all your heart, and not to know how to move on. I thought, Hey! That's me. Then I really slowed down. In fact, I bent over and did some stretches and lunges 'til they walked past me. Trailing about ten feet behind them, I moseyed along, close enough to hear. (Fine. I was eavesdropping. It happens to the best of us.) This is what blew my mind. The crying woman said, "I've got to get some single friends. But even if I could pull myself together enough to go out for a drink and leave the kids with a sitter, who would I go out with? Everyone I know is married." I wanted to yell up to her, "Hey, I'm in the same boat. It sucks. I get it. I have no life." I wanted her to know that I had these same problems, that we are all the same woman, that the things we think separate us—age, lifestyle, politics, religion—don't. Inside we are all still trying to find the balance of who we are as women. Are we sexy in our lingerie or schlumpy in our sweats? How do we define ourselves—as a wife, a mother, a friend, and a lover all at the same time? This is what we share—the daily challenges of our identity—of who we are and what we want and how to get there.

My friend told me a story about dressing up like Medusa for Halloween. She had a wig on with snakes sewn onto it. That famous Medusa hair that's supposed to turn men to stone—in this case it was turning a guy on instead. She was at a party and some guy was flirting with her all night. He kept saying he wanted to see her without her wig. She was happy to take it off. It was heavy and hot. But when she came out of the bathroom the guy took one look at her and said, "Oh. I recognize you now. We've met before." Then he disappeared, never to be seen again. Here's the truth. What you see isn't what you get. People see glamorous photos of me in magazines and assume I have it easy. But you should know that those pictures, where I'm heavily made up, standing under giant hot lights, dressed in clothes I don't own, and, more importantly, cut and airbrushed to impossible perfection, don't tell the whole story. Just because I look good in a magazine doesn't mean I feel confident about being naked in front of a man (especially when it's the first time that I'm naked in front of him). When you establish a mythical image—of your doing or not—you have to deal with the potential letdown in the harsh light of reality.

I, like Medusa, know a thing or two about fake hair. I don't get extensions, but for photo shoots or events they'll clip in extra layers of glossy locks. It makes your hair look thicker. I've never actually gone on a date like that, but even at an event, if someone even comes near putting his hand on my hair, I'm like, "Don't touch me!" And God forbid an event should actually turn into a date. I'd have to go into the bathroom and take a quarter of my hair out. And then what would I do with all that extra hair? Stick it in my purse—that tiny, very practical Judith Leiber bag (I actually adore her bags, one of which, by total coincidence, is called the "Emerson Rose") that's big enough for a credit card, a key, and a lipstick? Then I'd inevitably reach in for my lipstick and accidentally pull out a hairball. What a turn-on.

You know, I've got to tell you that this sort of happened to me the other night. I was at a party and met a really cute, charismatic man. It was the first time in a long while that I'd felt the little tingling feeling you get when you might like to go out with a guy or get to know him better. Well, he went to touch my hair, and since I'd just come from a magazine cover shoot, I had those thickening hairpieces clipped in. He felt them, and I backed away sort of embarrassed. He said, "Is that a wig?" And I ran into the bathroom and took them out. Of course I didn't have a Judith Leiber bag so I had to put the hair in the garbage, and it's expensive. Completely humiliated, I went out to talk to him and I could tell the moment had been singed. So you tell me—was it good news or bad when the next day I found out from a friend that he didn't remember meeting me anyway? And you wonder why I don't have a boyfriend.

Vulnerability is human. It's where we expose our true selves and pray that people won't use it against us. Sometimes I think couples ought to have to fight that way. You know, naked. The woman yelling,

"I can't believe you went out with the boys again." And then the guy coming back with, "Well, I can't believe you spent three hundred dollars on a pair of shoes." Okay, now take off your clothes and say that again.

I guess this is why those magazines upset me so much. This isn't just a tabloid Hollywood thing. Our society thrives on schadenfreude, the fancy German way of saying we take pleasure from other people's pain. I don't get why we continue to expect things from ourselves and our government, like world peace and the end of global warming, when we're snarky and gossipy and competitive. It's not about reading hurtful gossipy magazines that hurt famous strangers we've never met. The real problem is what we learn from that experience.

When I explain the tabloids to Emerson, I say, "I guess they just want to know that we're like them." What I don't say to her is that they want to catch celebrities doing something wrong. Looking fat. Having a wardrobe malfunction. Choking on a french fry. These are not stories of hope or inspiration. They're not stories we relate to. They're just images of some poor misguided girl caught wearing the wrong dress. By reading that crap, we develop a taste for judging others. We check out people's cellulite in magazines, then bring that attitude into our lives. We gossip about our friends and judge them. As long as people are buying the worst of the tabloids—two-headed-baby ones where everything isn't true—and those publishers are making money by running photos of cellulite butts, they're going to keep having their photographers follow people around. I have no way of changing this element of society, but I wish I could. That's why I bother to email the tabloids. In my little way I want to do my part to stop this from going unchecked. It's hurtful to other women. We struggle so hard to be comfortable in our bodies. Magazines don't need to perpetuate self-doubt and to associate value with skin tone and breast size. So this is my crack at encouraging you to stop buying junky gossip rags. I can't do it alone with my paltry email campaign. Stopping the negative tabloid coverage is like trying to stop drug trafficking. It will never succeed until the consumer stops buying it—stops wanting it. It damages us more than we realize to read false (occasionally true, but mostly false) versions of other people's misery and hardships. Don't do it for the "poor" celebrities. Do it for yourself and your daughters.

In spite of all my efforts to put external judgments aside, I can still focus on the negative like everybody else. Being naked is especially scary. Even at one of those Korean natural mineral spas where everyone is naked, I feel the impulse to hide my body. I just sit in there, two hot Jacuzzis to my right, steam room and sauna to the left. The place is filled with women, some of whom have way saggier boobs than mine, but I'm the one wearing a thin little coverup. I don't feel comfortable sitting naked. Then I look up and see a plaque on the spa's bathroom wall. It's a quote from Mother Teresa. It says, SPREAD LOVE EVERYWHERE YOU GO: FIRST OF ALL IN YOUR OWN HOME. GIVE LOVE TO YOUR CHILDREN, TO YOUR WIFE OR HUSBAND, TO A NEXT DOOR NEIGHBOR . . . LET NO ONE EVER COME TO YOU WITHOUT LEAVING BETTER AND HAPPIER. BE THE LIVING EXPRESSION OF GOD'S KINDNESS; KINDNESS IN YOUR FACE, KINDNESS IN YOUR EYES, KINDNESS IN YOUR SMILE, KINDNESS IN YOUR WARM GREETING. Me and my self-consciousness. Enough of that. Accepting oneself is a journey. The more you let go of your hang-ups, the more time you have for love, kindness, and generosity. Last time I needed the robe, maybe next time I won't. And maybe by the time after that, this book will have been published and I'll have helped someone else to feel comfortable with her body.

Here's my fantasy. I dream that someone will love me as a person so wholly that it won't matter whether I have gray pubic hair or sagging breasts. I dream this for all of us. Let's try to help our daughters escape the insecurities that plague us. Let's teach our sons to love women for their hearts and minds. Let's be grateful for bras, but let's find ways to be comfortable with our aging, naked bodies instead of deeming them flawed. Let's resist the urge to condemn others to make ourselves feel better. Instead, let's join forces to support all women—fat, thin, hairy, bald, short, tall, graying, saggy, and sun-scarred—no matter what container they come in. No matter how easy it looks on the surface, we're all living real, human lives, and everyone has it hard in one way or another. We have to remember that and be gentle to each other because of it. As for the pretty fish that Emerson caught—we ate it. Do I feel bad about that? Not really. At least when we ate the pretty thing we were nourished with protein and omega-3 and pride. But on some level I do understand how it felt.

Once Burnt, Twice Shy

You have to take risks if you want to accomplish anything in life. You have to ask that cute guy in the flower shop for his phone number. You have to buy a lottery ticket. You have to send a résumé to your dream job. Life doesn't happen unless you take chances. I think of one Easter when I was making dinner for twenty-two people. It was a big menu—Cornish game hen, biscuits, green beans, asparagus, ham, salad—and I enlisted my dad, who's a great cook, to help me out in the kitchen while my mother took care of Emerson. Dad was officially making the scalloped potatoes, a favorite from his southern Oklahoma childhood, but it was an elaborate meal and I needed help with the multitudinous other dishes. I was working on the asparagus, the ham, and the salad, and I ended up delegating a bit more to my dad than he bargained for. After cleaning the hens and washing and chopping the green beans, he got a late start on his special potatoes.

Unbeknownst to me, scalloped potatoes are a fairly complicated dish. There was lots of peeling and prep to be done. It got later and later and closer and closer to dinnertime. Finally, the pressure became too much, and my dad threw up his arms. He said, "I'm not doing this anymore," and left the house. Suddenly, my support staff (Dad) was gone and I was cooking the huge meal alone. Ack. The potatoes were already in a bowl of milk. I had no idea where he was in the recipe or what to do with them, so in a very anti–Martha Stewart way, I just dumped some water in with the milk and boiled them. When they were soft enough, I threw them in the blender and then mashed them. In the middle of this seat-of-the-pants mayhem I reached into the oven to get the Cornish game hens. Youch! Who knows what I was doing or how I did it, but I burnt myself. Now a big, angry, blistering burn was rudely announcing itself on my arm. Just what I needed. I barely paused. There wasn't time to curse, plus it was Easter. So no time for ice; I just kept going.

It's an indisputable fact that the oven is a useful kitchen device with many fine features. You can control the level and direction of heat while preserving nutrients and flavor. And, unlike a microwave, it doesn't turn everything to unevenly heated mush. A brilliant invention. But here's the catch (there's always a catch): The oven will burn you. It is a hazardous appliance. It's like a tiger. You can live with it for years without trouble until you're convinced it's tame, then out of the blue—it attacks. But the oven isn't the unpredictable factor. It's you. Burns happen when you're frazzled and moving too quickly for the situation. You burn yourself in chaos. You have to turn on the oven and chance getting burnt, because if you proceed with caution, the result will be delicious and relatively pain-free. It's the same thing in life and love. If you're willing to take risks, sometimes they pay off. I served those slapdash Oklahoma-scalloped-meets-LA-blended potatoes for Easter dinner, and they ended up being the best mashed potatoes anyone had ever had. Even when things go wrong, when you suffer a burn or change recipes on the fly, you have more chances for success than you think. Sure, I'll have that Easter dinner scar on my arm for the rest of my life. But every scar is a lesson. The ones on my knees remind me not to fall off my bike—even if I don't have that problem so much anymore.

Seriously, if you notice lots of bruises on your body—if you keep having that experience where you're rounding a corner and you don't quite judge it right so you hit your shoulder on the wall—then you're just like me, 'cause that's what I do when I'm too cluttered, too hurried, too scattered. Your body is calling out for your attention. Either it will get sick, or you'll start slipping and banging into things. The message is simple: Slow down.

The oven burn on my arm reminds me to move slowly and cautiously, but also to remain hopeful. When you've been through a divorce or two (who's counting?), it's tough to find hope. Dating again is scary. It's hard to imagine sharing your life, but equally awful is the idea of not sharing it. It's hard to trust your heart, and it's hard to trust other people. Like they say, once bitten, twice shy. Or—if we want to stick to the oven metaphor—once burnt, twice shy. And when you've been twice burnt, well, the shyness tends to compound almost exponentially. (Told you I was a math person.)

The last time I took Emerson in for a checkup, her pediatrician took me aside afterward. After saying nice things about Emerson, he asked, "What about you? How are you?" I said I was fine. Then he asked if I was in a relationship. And I had to admit that I hadn't been on a date in months. I thought he wanted to set me up on a blind date or something, but he said, quite firmly, "You should date. Emerson needs a healthy model for relationships." Yikes. Sure, your girlfriends might say, "You should get out there. There are tons of great men." But when it comes from your child's pediatrician, when the doctor's orders are to get a life for your daughter's sake? Now that's a wake-up call. I realized that yes, it's great that Emerson's seen me survive and thrive on my own, but I want her to see me needing somebody, trusting somebody, giving myself over to somebody. I want her to see me doing it well—loving and being loved.

Ah, yes, my dating life. This is the part of the book that I'm sure the tabloids will mutilate and regurgitate in the form of headlines about this "desperate" woman and her "tell-all" about orgies. But really I'm just a forty-year-old single mom whose daughter's pediatrician told her to date, and who wanted to, but was shy. People expect that if you're pretty, successful—whatever—the boyfriend mission should be easy. *Should* is the key word. The other moms at Emerson's school know me well enough to see that I never go anywhere with a guy, and I sure mustn't have one hidden somewhere or I wouldn't have time to bake 250 cookies for the school's fiftieth anniversary party. (That's it! My secret lover—the KitchenAid mixer!) When I tell people I don't date, they assume it's because men are intimidated by me. But my dating troubles aren't because I'm a celebrity. It's just the normal girly struggle of not knowing how to meet someone. I don't know who the right guy is. I'm swamped with so many tasks, from work to taking the trash cans out, that I don't make time to go out. (And by the way, I'm a traditionalist enough to still feel that putting out the trash is a man's job. Right along with lightbulb changing and toilet plunging. So even though I can do those things, and I do do those things, if Mr. Right is reading this, he should consider himself duly notified.) I also can't tell if someone is interested in me. And I spend time thinking about what they might not like about me instead of determining what I actually think of them.

Yeah—I'm not the best advisor when it comes to dating. Since being single I've made my share of mistakes. But that makes me extremely well qualified to tell you what *not* to do. Here goes:

First of all, don't date millionaire coke addicts. If you want to connect with another person, you have to expose some of yourself, and I'm not talking about skin. Admitting to hopes and fears is what makes us feel understood. It's what makes us human. Going on a date makes you instantly vulnerable. Last year a friend set me up on a blind date with a millionaire guy. He was six foot three, had dark curly hair, and had never been married. He had a plane. He spoke French. This was a dating first for me. I'd never dated anyone that fancy before. We went to dinner three times, and I didn't sleep with him or anything like that. I'm slow to trust, and I was kind of afraid of getting intimate with him.

I didn't exactly hide my fears from the millionaire. Far from it. I told him, "You're expecting some glamorous Teri Hatcher, and when I take off my clothes I'm just going to be me. And in the morning I'm going to be me with bad hair." I'm not like my *Desperate Housewives* character Susan as a mom, but we have this insecurity in common. Susan hasn't picked good men, and I haven't either—even if they were good people, they weren't good for me. I guess I have trust issues. I don't have faith that I'll find a happy relationship, that it will work out. Behaving that way creates a self-fulfilling prophecy. It's not a black-and-white thing—you're a secure person or you're an insecure person. We all have layers of personality that support and conflict with each other. I'm a survivor at my core, but coating that is a layer of insecurity from messages I got as a child. And coating that is my perfectionism. And beyond the perfectionist is the fear of doing something wrong. These layers peel and reveal themselves in the course of a day. That's how we struggle with our insecurities—in bits and pieces, in moments and situations. (And it explains the smell that people keep thinking is *eau d'onion*.) We bounce between self-doubt and self-assurance. I'm never a total mushball, but I'm not a ball of confidence either. Trusting men is a hard thing for me. Like Susan, I want to have faith, but I waver. It's probably why I'm not in a successful relationship.

As it happened, the millionaire never got to experience my morning hairdo. Just when I started to open up a little bit, he "forgot" a date we had planned. Then he got all defensive about it. And then he accused me of overreacting. I've been honest enough with you for 141 pages, so I know you'll believe me when I say—*I didn't overreact*. Basically, he turned into an unfamiliar freak. On top of this, I found out that he was already in a long-term relationship—with cocaine. As soon as I see anything like that, I'm outta there. When this information flooded in, I did something new and bold for me. I can be one of those nonconfrontational people who never calls the guy back or just sort of gets mad and hangs up. But this time I knew what I didn't want so clearly that I calmly told him, "You know what? This isn't going to work for me. I wish you luck and happiness, but I'm not able to do this with you." He was stunned. I think millionaires with planes aren't used to getting the door slammed—they're used to slamming it themselves. The next day he sent me the meanest email I'd ever gotten in my life. Among other things, it said, "And you're right. You probably *don't* look good in the morning." Yeah, sometimes being honest can really come back to bite you in the ass.

Second, don't mingle with a writer who has a live-in girlfriend. You know how when you first start to date someone, you don't have an immediate right to ask if they're seeing anyone? I mean, I guess you can ask if they're married or have a serious girlfriend, but isn't that the same thing as asking, "Are you a cheating jerk?" And if they're casually dating other people, well, that's fair. They're allowed. You're not in a relationship yet. So when this writer said he was "kinda seeing someone" I figured, okay, he has a dating life. I don't, but good for him.

Well, later that night we walked out of a club, and the next morning there we were—front-page news. I felt bad. I'd had no idea that there were paparazzi outside. When I called him to apologize, he said that, boy, was his girlfriend pissed. She was moving out. It turned out that he had been living with someone for two years! He sounded devastated, and I felt terrible that I'd caused this rift. Then I realized that he'd deceived me. He'd gone on a date with me when he had a live-in girlfriend. And there I was, feeling like it was *my* fault. So when you ask a guy if he's seeing someone and he says, "Well, a little," multiply by ten. I sure can pick 'em.

Third, avoid men who have stock in hookers. Seriously, it was my misfortune that a man I met one night and talked to for three hours (it was a stimulating conversation) turned out to have an addiction to, shall we say, the pay-me-for-sex type of woman. Not that I'm judging that, but like I said, when I see something wrong, well, I wasn't about to stick around to see if he joined HOHA (and I don't mean a comedy troupe, I mean Hooked On Hookers Anonymous).

Fourth, avoid any man whose primary interest is finding someone to propagate his seed. People say that at a certain age, women start hearing the ticking of their biological clocks, but it happens to the men too. There was one guy I dated a few times who came to a party I was hosting. In the middle of the party, when I was greeting people and making sure everyone had drinks and checking to see that there was still toilet paper in the bathroom, he cornered me and held forth about how he wanted me to have his child. It was completely out of the blue. He skipped all the dating, the getting serious, the falling in love, the lingering nights spent comparing hopes and fantasies, the part where I make sure he likes dogs and isn't allergic to my slowly dying cats, and cut right to the part where I bear his children. If his goal was to sweep me off my feet, well, he failed. And in doing so left me with yet another dating failure for my list.

Before I got married to Emerson's father, I was involved for a long time with a guy who didn't want to be in a committed relationship. He didn't want to be monogamous. We went back and forth about what we were and what we could or should be for a while, until finally I bailed. I told him I couldn't do the casual relationship thing and that I was done. A few months passed during which, as it happened, I met someone else. Of course, as soon as that happened, he started calling. A lot. It was a classic case of too little too late, and I didn't return his calls. The messages became increasingly urgent. When he finally reached me, he announced, "I want to be with someone I can trust and someone with whom I can have a baby." I said, "Listen to what you just said. You want to be with someone. *Someone.* Not me." He trusted me. Check. I was female and therefore could probably bear him a child. Check. It was a very short, impersonal list of criteria and I fulfilled it. I guess there's just a breed of men who, around the age of forty, realize they want kids. The thing is, they've gone a long time without a wife, and they actually still don't want one. I guess instinctual urges to further their genes must take over, because somehow they actually believe a woman would be satisfied with being one step above "egg donor."

Okay, here's a good one. My friend Val had a houseguest—a friend of a friend whom her husband had crossed paths with years earlier. He was heir to an oil fortune and had come to LA to invest in movies. I met him over at Val's house and we started talking about business ideas. He seemed interested in some of the projects I'd been working on and asked if we could continue the conversation over dinner. I didn't know if it was supposed to be a date, but Val and I decided I had nothing to lose. I was fresh off the divorce—I needed to get myself out there. And this guy was a potential investor. How bad could it be? But the night of the date I got a phone call from Val. She said, "I've got good news and bad news, which do you want first?" Of course I wanted the bad news. She said, "Well, the bad news is I'm calling to break your date."

Why was Val calling, instead of my would-be suitor/investor? Apparently, as the date approached, Val's houseguest got a little stranger. He said he didn't like public spaces and wanted to rent out an entire restaurant for our dinner. So, Val later told me, he was in the kitchen researching venues and calling caterers when the doorbell rang. It was FedEx with a package. Val had her hands full with the kids and asked this guy to go down and get the package. He left, but ten minutes later he hadn't returned. She went downstairs and found half the LAPD in the driveway. She thought she was being punk'd, but no. My date was under arrest. He was a con artist who had been fraudulently raising money and living on scams. Wow. I said, "I see. And what's the good news?" She said, "The good news is that he's in jail and will never be able to bother you or me again." He was arrested while he was booking the date with me.

It's funny now, sure, but at the time I didn't really see the humor. It was my first post-divorce foray into dating and it was exactly the wrong start. Talk about trust issues. Imagine if the first man who asks you out after your divorce is a con artist. Okay, so my fifth piece of dating advice is easy. Take it from me: Don't date con artists.

Sixth, and this one may be tempting, but the pitfalls are obvious: Don't accept money for dates. The same matchmaker friend who set me up with the millionaire coke addict went on to set me up with a creepy lawyer (yes, she and I are still friends, but she'll never live these dates down and she knows it). I spent less than an hour having dinner with him. It wasn't a match. No big deal. We said a polite good-night and that was that. Or so I thought. A few weeks later he called the house, got my assistant on the phone, and asked her to offer me $50,000 to go to a convention with him. (Wait, wasn't rule number three to avoid men who pay for sex . . . why is this becoming a theme for me?) He wanted to pay me the big bucks—like an escort! Who does that? Who has dinner with someone and then thinks, *Well, there was no chemistry, but for $50,000 maybe she'd be my arm candy.* Needless to say, my assistant firmly declined the offer. This guy had the nerve to ask if she could at least communicate the offer to me. My assistant said, "The answer is no. I don't need to consult Teri." At least I surround myself with intelligent people.

Even though I won't accept $50,000 for a date, I'll admit that I do care about money. But not for shallow reasons. I was sitting on the beach in Malibu with a few friends, and a very attractive man walked past. The girls were talking about how hot he was. One of their husbands came over and even he had to admit that this guy was really good looking. Another husband stepped in to say that he knew him and he was really nice. And then my friend Tara* said, "And he's rich too!" I perked up. "He's rich?" It was like an antenna popped out of my head. My friends wouldn't stop teasing me about it. I protested—I was reacting to the idea that he was handsome and nice *and* rich. I'm not a gold digger! But rich—or let's say financially secure—had a nice ring to it and I'll tell you why.

I've always been a romantic. Even when I was a teenager, I'd go on a single date with a guy and the next thing you knew I'd be testing out the sound of "Mrs. Teri Winklesmith." My fantasy went right to marriage, and as we now know from the oven story, moving too fast can be dangerous. I never allowed myself to go slow and question and learn and be aware of what was happening. I had my Snow White fantasy, and I superimposed it on every relationship. Even if he obviously wasn't Prince Charming, it was easier and more satisfying to imagine that he was. I ignored the rough edges of our relationships, hoping that time and wishfulness would smooth them away. The result was that my relationships were more about the fantasy of love than the actual day-to-day experience of it. Whole romances fabricated out of air. I lost chunks of my life to those delusions.

Still, it's not like I married the first bozo who came along. After coming out of that relationship with the guy who slept with all of France, all I cared about was not getting hurt. I didn't care about our sex life or his finances. I picked nice guys. But at the wise age of forty, I now know that finding someone who isn't going to hurt you isn't exactly setting the bar high. A lifelong relationship needs more than that. Nice isn't enough.

I've taken care of everyone my whole life—emotionally as a kid, and financially as a young adult. I've never had a guy support me—ever. I never lived in anyone else's house. I always paid the rent, handled the bills, purchased the wedding presents for our friends, pulled

---

*Just to remind you that Tara isn't her real name. But he *was* really rich.

out my credit card after dinner. I bought them thoughtful and/or expensive birthday presents and Christmas presents and Valentine's Day gifts. So now I'd like to try a role reversal. You know, a little taste of traditionalism where I get to be the girl and he gets to be the guy. I take care of him, he pays for things (and takes out the trash and changes the lightbulbs, like I said before).

Traditionalism brings me to jewelry. And on this subject I think there are two kinds of women—the women who get jewelry from men, and those who do not. I know, I know—I can't exactly claim this phenomenon exists or has relevance in third world countries. It's shallow by definition. But in our own, small, personal worlds, it's worth exploring. Why? Because it unveils a male-female dynamic that has relevance in our daily lives. I'm the second kind of woman. The kind who never gets trinkets from the man of the moment. I've always wondered why. It's a very traditional gift in this country. Women in relationships get jewelry from men every now and then. I had to ask, "Is there something about me that says, 'Nah, don't get her jewelry?'"

In my early twenties, I used to actually say, "I'm not that into diamonds." Can you imagine?! But it was more complicated than that. It seemed wrong to want men to give me luxury gifts. I mean, being given flowers was one thing. But jewelry seemed so grown-up and serious, and to want it seemed to verge on sexist. What did a necklace mean? Was it too expensive? Did it make a relationship more serious than it actually was? Did it symbolize some kind of ownership that he had over you? For me there's always a little bit of tension between wanting to be taken out to dinner, treated like a lady, etc., and not wanting to feel like a trophy, to feel bought, or to feel like the money he spends on you creates some sort of obligation.

A man who lived across the world recently offered to fly me to London for a date. (Talk about long-distance dating. You know you're in trouble if a ten-hour flight is how you meet halfway.) His invitation was at once entrancing—I loved the idea that he would go to great lengths and expense to see me. But it was also appalling—and not just because every time I fly I think I'm going to die. (I mean, the whole man-can-fly thing just seems so wrong, and who really understands how a plane works anyway? I always thought it was that the engines pushed so hard that it went really fast and the wind underneath lifted the wings. Now they tell me it's about suction—that the speed creates a vacuum that lifts the plane. Either way, I don't get it. All I know is I go on, I eat peanuts, I sit in a chair that crooks my neck forward uncomfortably, and I endure hours of anxiety only moderately quelled by an after-liftoff Bloody Mary and, with luck, a cute guy in conversational range.)

But back to the cross-continental date. The real reason it was appalling, certain plane-crash death aside, was that it was such a horrible waste of money. To this particular guy (like the women who buy the $20,000 dresses) the money was irrelevant. Or so he claimed. But what would I owe him in return? Doesn't a round-trip first-class ticket to London imply more than a peck on the cheek? I worried that he'd expect me to sleep with him, which I definitely wasn't going to do. I asked a friend whether she thought that was part of the deal. She said, "Absolutely not! You'll stay in separate rooms. His reward for flying you to London is your company over dinner. If he wants to sleep with you it's going to take a lot more than a plane trip." She was kidding, of course. There's no date/sex exchange rate. But gifts are tricky. You have to be careful. That's why it seems safer to pay your own way. To let him know by your actions that you can take care of yourself. You don't need him to provide for you or treat you to dinner or to give you presents. You're two independent grown-ups who don't need materialist symbols of one another's affections. Yeah, right.

So why do I send the "thanks, but no thanks" message? Why is it so much harder to receive than it is to give? In a relationship—and I think this happens mostly to women—you get sucked into feeling like yes, you'd like your husband or boyfriend to help you out, but it'll be faster and easier to do it yourself. Maybe it's finding an apartment to rent. Maybe it's cleaning the house or packing for a trip or getting the kids to bed. Even if he's willing to help, what are the chances that he's going to do it the way you want it done? He'll forget to ask if the apartment has a dishwasher. Or he'll forget to pack the kids' bathing suits. It's just easier to do it yourself. If the goal is speed, you may be right. But is that the only goal? What about the balance of the relationship? What are you sacrificing by doing it yourself (besides your own free time)? If you give your spouse the opportunity to participate, the thing will get done, and it will be okay. It might be different than you would do it—you might have to buy a replacement bathing suit for the kid—but he'll feel needed and important. Just like the way I let my daughter tie her own shoes. (Not to imply that all men are seven-year-olds. Oh, what the hell, yes they are.) And letting him be a real part of the relationship is more important than getting the thing done quickly and right. It all comes back to vulnerability. In a long-term relationship you have to relinquish control. You have to let yourself need someone else. You have to let him feel needed.

That's something I'll admit to failing at doing in my marriage. I've never been very good at letting people help me. When Jon and I were living in New York, we'd walk out of the apartment and I'd be carrying the twenty-pound stroller and the diaper bag full of bottles and snacks under one arm and Emerson under the other. Jon would say, "Let me take something," but I'd say, "No problem. I got it." I didn't show him that I needed him. I couldn't trust him—I was too scared of being let down. It was also kind of arrogant—feeling like my way was the best and I didn't want anyone to stand in my way. I could have let him feel more needed, but I was too afraid. It was too hard for me to trust. This isn't great for a man or a marriage. Even my girlfriends noticed the luggage thing, so much so that on a recent trip to London my friend said, "And Teri, don't pick up your luggage because once you do no one at the hotel will offer to help you again." She was right. I couldn't stop myself, and sure enough I became the lady who carried it all by herself even on the other side of the Atlantic.

That attitude of complete self-reliance has its benefits, to be sure. I never took my Prince Charming fantasy so far that I became a helpless, passive sleeping beauty, waiting to be rescued. Because lying there for a hundred years without aging only happens in books. But my self-reliance has deprived me, most certainly, of some very fine jewelry. I'm too busy proving my independence. Great. Look how independent I am now. The goal is to find your perfect balance. You don't want to be a diamond slut, purposefully walking your spouse past the window of Zales every time you leave the house. But show your need. Communicate your desires. Allow yourself to be adored and adorned. Let yourself feel like you deserve it. Show your faith in his taste. Show him you can learn things from him.

I'm telling you this, but I haven't succeeded at it yet. It's a goal for my next relationship. If you try it more, I promise I will too. Probably what will happen for me is that the pendulum will swing the other way entirely. I'm going to break my old habits, like pulling out my credit card after every meal. I'm not paying for any more dinners, dammit! I'm absolutely done taking care of men. I want to be someone's girlfriend or wife, not his mother. I want to lie on a sofa and have grapes dropped into my mouth while my feet are being rubbed. Oh, wait, did I say that? That may be taking it too far.

Oh yeah—I almost forgot. If you do let yourself become the jewelry getter, and you get some, well listen up. I have a tip from my friend Lori, whose husband has been known to give her a jewel or two. In spite of whatever signals I was giving out, one particularly brave soul was moved to give me a lovely bracelet. I was touched, and told my friend Lori about it. The next time I saw her, she looked at my wrist and exclaimed, "Where's the bracelet?"

"Oh, I'm not wearing it," I said. "I don't wear jewelry that often." She shook her head in despair.

"Listen," she said. "You want more jewelry? You wear what he gives you."

Having a child makes it easier to see and admit these failings. You start to think about what you want your child's experience of relationships to be. You think about how she's going to be treated. Seeing the world as a mother has allowed me to change significantly. I stopped trying to be the "hero," who did everything herself. Being right all the time kept me safe. Safe from needing anyone else and safe from disappointment. But now I'm strong enough to face the possibility of disappointment and to weather it when it comes about. I don't need to protect myself, so I'm open to failing. And I've stopped feeling like my way is the only way to do things. It's not just that I think this with my head. I've come to feel it in my heart. Needing someone else breeds and fosters love, trust, and a partnership that lasts. I even notice the change at work. If a director asks me to try a different way of doing a scene, even if I don't agree, I'll try it his way, and I'll give it my all because a) he deserves the respect and b) I could be wrong. Yep. I could be wrong. Being wrong doesn't wound me like it used to. It doesn't completely destroy my "perfect" façade. It lets me know that I'm fallible, that I can use help, that I can ask for it, and that, most of all, I'm human.

No matter what I think I want in a man, finding the right person always comes back to vulnerability, to being willing to turn on the oven and risk the burn. You need to learn to pay attention to your instincts and to trust them. Remember when Emerson busted me trying to clean out the medicine cabinet? I stopped what I was doing and read her book about the night sky with her. We lay flat on her bed with the book in front of us. There were drawings of the constellations in the southern hemisphere. We tried to guess what they were. We're not talking Big Dipper or Orion's Belt. We're talking random connect-the-dots, drawings that could be a king or a house or Duchamp's *The Bride Stripped Bare by Her Bachelors, Even*. We came to one—a group of nine stars that looked to me like a dying cow. I kept quiet, waiting for

Emerson to make her guess. She shook her head. She had no idea what it was. I explained to her that there was no right answer—some ancient Greek astronomer had decided what he thought it was and now she could do the same. There was a long pause. Then she shrugged and said, "Fine. It's a man holding a bucket of water." We were surprised to discover that she was right. It was Aquarius, the Water Bearer. Emerson said, "I was just joking. I didn't really think that." I told her that she shouldn't be so hesitant to say what she thinks. "You know a lot," I told her. "You don't need to doubt yourself." I told her she should trust her instincts. We all should.

Where were my instincts when I dated the lying writer and the coked-up millionaire? Well, those issues weren't exactly subtle. They revealed themselves pretty quickly, and in my own defense I'll say that as soon as they were apparent, I was done. I cut my losses. In cases like that, there's still a little burn from the oven, but it fades quickly and leaves no scar. But I know I have good instincts buried under my bad choices. Hey, I once stopped at a green light because I had a sense that a guy in an SUV was going to run the red. Indeed he did. Gavin De Becker wrote a whole book called *The Gift of Fear* about how we can and should trust our gut instincts for when we're in danger. Like the time I was mugged. There was a second between seeing the bad guy and having him point the gun at my face when I sensed something was wrong—only in that case it was too late to cross the street. I like to believe the gift of fear works the other way too. Call it the gift of trust. Let's have faith that if we pay close attention to our instincts, we'll know who deserves our trust when they come along.

In dating and in all relationships—with friends and family and colleagues and employees—you have to work on choosing the right people, recognizing your allies, and knowing whom to trust. I've had friends that I needed to weed out, like a garden. It's such a tough thing. I had a good, old friend. I knew in my heart that she was a good person, a well-intentioned person, but I came to realize that she wasn't good for me. She was critical and judgmental and opinionated. That's a great friend-match for someone who's flighty and unrealistic, but I'm too much of a realist as it is. I judge myself enough as it is. I don't need a friend shouting, "More! More!" when I'm so hard on myself already. It's painful to let go, but sometimes you have to do it.

You also have to work on your own issues in relationships. It's your insecurities and fears that lead you to the wrong people. Within the relationship, you have to be willing to trust; you have to turn on the oven and start cooking. There are no written instructions for making this meal. Once you've started, you have to move cautiously, to know your own limits, to be spontaneous (throw the potatoes in the blender!), and to follow your instincts (add spice!). Above all, you have to let yourself be vulnerable. The only way to find a real connection is to let people see the real you, layers of insecurity and all.

There are bound to be burns along the way. I'd been on five or six dates with a guy who wasn't my lover, much less my boyfriend. I told you! I'm slow! Slow is good, remember? But I am an adult, and I'm not a virgin (the daughter should have been a clue). We were at dinner, at a quiet Italian restaurant, and we were talking about deep stuff. He was challenging me to be open and to take risks in a kind of flirty, sexual way. And I want to be like that, to trust someone. So as we were having dessert, he asked, "What do you want to do after dinner?" I wanted to be feminine and sexy with this person, so I did it. I jumped off the cliff. No waffling, no dillydallying. I took a huge risk and plunged off my own personal biker-below-be-damned precipice of fear and distrust and said, "I want you to take me to a store and buy me beautiful lingerie, and then I want to go back to your place and model it for you." After the words came out of my mouth I was so proud of myself that I practically leapt on my chair to take a bow. Except that such a public display would be a whole other cliff. One cliff per night is my limit.

Surprise, surprise, my date liked my suggestion. The only store open at that time was the Hustler store on Sunset Boulevard that, turns out, has some very nice, non-trashy lingerie. We made a few purchases and brought the goods back to his place. I put on a simple black negligee and, I have to say, I felt good. I'm pretty sure I looked good too. It made me feel sexy. And I think that's why I jumped off the cliff. Being open, tonight at least, included being sexually confident. We started making out. Things were hot and heavy until . . . let's just say that, for my friend, it was over before it even began. Haste made waste. The wine was sold before its time. It was over before the (not) fat lady sang. Get the picture?

He didn't say anything about his little accident (so much for openness). I was okay with it, even a bit flattered. I thought we could just . . . start over. But his energy had shifted. He said, "I'm tired, and you need to go." I figured he was embarrassed, so I didn't try to make him talk about it. I left.

A week later I was home with the flu. He called and said, "Hi, this is Tom Winklesmith." (Name changed to protect the sexually incompetent.) He gave his last name too. As if I didn't know which Tom I'd made out with whilst garbed in sexy lingerie the week prior. I playfully teased him. "Yeah, I think I know your last name!" But he cut me short. He said, "I thought you deserved to know that I got back together with my ex-girlfriend." Whoa. This was completely out of the blue. I hadn't even known there was a significant ex, much less one who was ripe for reunion. When I hung up the phone I burst into tears. That motherfucker. I opened myself up and what did I get? Scorched.

I rallied a couple girlfriends for burn-victim treatment. One of my girlfriends, Lisa, just said, "He probably went back to his girlfriend because she's not as hot as you—so he won't get overexcited." Another one of my girlfriends is a bit more big-picture. You know—India yoga kind of big-picture. Maya said (as she has before and probably will again), "It isn't about him and what a jerk he is. It's about you. It's about what you did. It's about how you, knowing yourself, jumped off the cliff. You opened up. You went for it and didn't hide your feelings.

Good for you! Someday you're going to do that and the guy's going to appreciate it. Forget him. You made progress." I knew she was right. Being vulnerable was my personal challenge, and I'd had a modicum of success. I could be proud of that in spite of the rejection.

Lisa had no patience for that kind of analysis. She pulled out a t-shirt that she'd made for me. It said, "I dated Tom Winklesmith and all I got was premature ejaculation." It's great to have both those friends—one to tell you your efforts weren't wasted and the other to make you laugh like a giggly teenager. We should have TP'd his house too!

I didn't exactly have a great track record for risk-taking. Back when I lived in North Hollywood, next door to the refrigeratorless Ned, there was a little window of time where it looked like we might date. One Presidents' Day weekend my dad had left his Jeep Cherokee with me—a rare luxury. Ned asked me to go to a movie—which he now says was a big deal for him. We had some extra time before the movie, so I suggested we go for a hike in Griffith Park. Halfway to the observatory at the top, the car conked out. We didn't have cell phones to call for help—this was back when cell phones still weighed ten pounds. (Okay, I'm dating myself, but hey, I've already admitted to being forty.) Remembering a gas station at the bottom of the hill, we walked down to it. The gas station had no tow truck. It was 5:30 on a Friday, not the best time to hunt down car help in LA. We called a few friends only to get answering machines about how lovers (it was also Valentine's Day) were out for the holiday. We decided we couldn't be too many miles from home so, making the best of it, we started to walk. Hell, we had wanted to hike anyway. You know how roads seem so close to each other when you're in a car, but then when you find yourself walking a familiar route, it's so long and slow and hot and devoid of sidewalks and utterly unscenic? That was us making our way west. It was a slog. Then we saw a bus coming by and thought, *Well, there's something we've never done in LA. Let's get on it.* We were sure it was heading the right way. But then it got on the freeway and I couldn't have pulled that emergency get-off wire faster. I feared we'd end up in Bakersfield, which in those days we thought was the armpit of California. The first stop was Burbank.

Now we were hot and tired and even farther from home, but the "I dare you to . . ." game had become a little exciting. Figuring it was a story we'd tell our kids one day, we walked into a liquor store, bought a couple beers, and drank them on the corner. While sitting there brown-bagging it, we realized we were closer to the Burbank airport than we were to our apartment, so we walked there to get a cab. But when we got to the airport we saw that there was a sixty-dollar round-trip flight to Vegas. Sixty dollars to Vegas! We could just go there. Ned and I always liked a challenge. This was the Vegas challenge. Who was going to say no? Which of us would back down? Ned told me that he knew of a Vegas hotel where you could get a free room if you were from Nebraska. Conveniently, he was from Nebraska. That sealed the deal. So we boarded a loud, unsettling prop plane that must've been from the war. I started hoping we'd win lots of money so we could take a real plane home.

When we got to Vegas, there was some kind of convention going on (biker conventions, Vegas conventions—I never get a room). All of Vegas was sold out. So much for spontaneity. We called hotels. We called the visitors' center. We'd been broken-down, lost, and walking aimlessly for hours and all I wanted to do was take a shower. I knew how the fun-loving and fancy-free girl would behave. She'd throw up her arms and say, "Who cares? It's Vegas! We'll gamble all night!" But I wasn't that girl. My knees were swollen and I was disappointed because any inkling I'd had that we might end up kissing in a room with a heart-shaped bed was out the window. Back then, I didn't handle disappointment too well. We decided to take the next flight out, but it wasn't until 6:30 A.M. Great. I was exhausted, and I was mad at Ned for dragging me on this ill-fated adventure. For his part, I'm sure he was annoyed that I was so petulant and high-maintenance. There was nothing to do but head to the blackjack table for a long night of gambling. I didn't enjoy it in the least. By the time we boarded the plane we were barely talking, and when we finally got home we went silently into our separate apartments. I tried to be spontaneous; look where it got me.

There's a happy end to the Vegas story. No, Ned and I weren't meant to be a couple. But we were meant to be lifelong friends. The deep, meaningful friendship that emerged after and in spite of that Vegas trip (and one other time when he called me flakey, which I found hard to forgive) is one of my most important. I'm so close to him and his family that he's Emerson's designated guardian if anything were ever to happen to me. And having that lousy night in Vegas, like a scar, adds character and texture and dimension to our teasing and friendship.

Even if you fail time after time (and I have), you need to keep taking risks. You need to be willing to need someone else. You need to have hope that one day you'll get the recipe just right. And when you make progress, you need to recognize it even if it doesn't yield the desired results. I have indeed made progress. For my fortieth birthday, someone gave me a very special gift. It was a silver harmonica from Tiffany's. It was my favorite gift. It seemed to encompass my personality perfectly—it was classic and simple, creative and down-to-earth. And it travels light (okay, that's not me). I have no idea how to play the harmonica, and that made it even better. It was my fortieth birthday, and it symbolized a fresh start. The best part of all was that it wasn't from a person who knew me well or had known me for a long time. It was from a person I work with, a member of the *Desperate Housewives* crew. So here was this person who only knew me from my behavior on the set, starting with the first episode of the show. Within that context—the context of my conduct at work and our friendly exchanges—he'd decided that this was the right gift for me. It meant so much to me. It felt like I was being recognized as myself—the way I see myself. I was coming across as the person I think I am and want to be. It was a great start to a new era.

Dare to Compare Apples and Oranges

Your friends cancel on you; your husband's playing poker; your kid's got a playdate—whatever it is, you suddenly have a free hour to yourself. How do you choose to spend the time? Here's what happens to me more often than not: My call time—the time I'm scheduled to show up on set—gets pushed an hour, and Emerson is still at school. What to do? Hmm. A bath would be nice. It would relax my shoulders. Very refreshing. Who doesn't love a bath? Or maybe I should lift weights instead. Also a good self-care option with possible side benefits of a firmer ass and flatter abs. Bath, weights, bath, weights. I can't decide. As these options run through my head, I sit at my computer mindlessly answering emails. Still pondering, I make the bed and refill the paper in the fax machine. Now fifteen minutes of my free hour are already gone and what do I have to show for it? Paper in the fax machine. God knows that's critical. What if I win the lottery and for some reason the only way they contact winners is via fax?

Okay, so I finally decide. A bath it is. Only now it'll have to be a forty-five-minute bath instead of an hour. I run the bath, and as the water pours into the tub, I grab a stack of unopened mail. A tree-trimmer's bill. A charity request. A California voter information guide. Valpak coupons, all right! Now the tub is ready, and I climb in with the voter guide—that way I can soak and study propositions at the same time. Relax without feeling wasteful. (Since when is it wasteful to take care of yourself?) I end up reading a measure on state spending and school funding limitations. Should the state continue to spend ninety billion dollars a year on education in spite of the budget shortfalls? I don't know! Should it? This seems like a lot of money and therefore a huge decision and I get caught up in plowing through all the fine print. Twenty-five minutes later I stop myself. I put down the papers. This isn't the relaxing bath I envisioned. I'm getting stressed out about the state of our public education. I need to clear my mind. I really need this bath. For myself. I add more hot water and sink low in the tub, with a glass of cool water at my side, candles lit, bath salts melting, and, finally, at last, I slowly begin to enjoy my—whoops, that's the doorbell. Better jump out and see who it is. Hour's up. Gotta go to work.

We have these choices all the time. Options present themselves and we waste time lingering on the decision, or we decide too fast, or we don't maximize the opportunity. We forget to relax in our baths. When I lie by the pool I keep thinking, *I should be swimming laps*. We listen to music when what we really need is silence. We check our email one more time even though we just looked at it two minutes earlier. We let the TV suck our lives away. These are the little decisions we make throughout every day. They don't seem like a big deal, but they are. I'll tell you why. The big decisions—getting married, taking a new job, buying a house, choosing a school for your kid—we know going into these moments that they're big. We stress about them. We plan for them. We research and deliberate and change our minds and lose sleep. They may not be easy decisions, but we're clear on one thing: They're important. But the little choices, they're the sneakier ones.

They don't announce themselves. They just creep in through the bathroom window so quietly that you don't even know they're there. And because they're so subtle, you can miss them altogether.

The little choices. Bath or exercise? Sleep in or vacuum? Cookies or carrots? Work late or leave now? Tell your husband you're grumpy or put on a good face? Answer the phone or let it ring? Dinner in front of the TV or at the table? There are hundreds of decisions that we face, as if they were new, time and time again. These are the moments that sculpt your life. They make you you. They add up to a lifetime. Like we talked about with dieting. One small decision to eat a pint of ice cream adds up to high cholesterol if you make that same choice every day. Or with your house. Buying it is the big decision, but choosing to ignore those nasty tree roots growing toward your pipes can lead to the explosion of raw sewage all over your floor. (Yeah, that happened to me. Pretty, huh?) Or with your career. My impulse to go to the *Love Boat* mermaid audition led to a big decision: dropping out of college. And twenty years later I'm dodging paparazzi instead of handing out homework.

So what am I saying? To make a big deal out of every little thing? Not exactly. But let's talk about dying. That's right, I want you to picture the end. No, not the end of this book. Our end. Yep, you and me, side by side in twin hospital beds. I've got an oxygen mask. You have a broken hip. But we both have long, thick, gorgeous hair. (It's the future—anything's possible!) We're on our deathbeds, and we're talking about what we wish we'd done differently. Dying is good if you don't regret how you lived. Well, maybe not *good*, but natural. And if you can die without saying, "I wish I'd tried that," then I guess you win. I sometimes think about how when I'm lying in my hospital bed and I know the end is near, I'll never say to myself, "Gosh, I wish I'd worked more hours." Or "Wow, I just wish I had more stuff." So when I'm lying there next to you (who knew we'd get to be such good friends?), I want to tell you that I don't have a single regret. I know my life may not have been perfect (especially if I can't afford a private hospital room), but I want to feel like I made each decision consciously and lovingly, and that even if things didn't come out great, I still did my best.

My days are full of what I guess you might call these Deathbed Decisions. Here's how the Deathbed Decisions work: In every small moment you just ask yourself, "On my deathbed, how will I wish I'd behaved?" Sound crazy? And morbid? But remember, your life is made up of those small moments. Your father never decided to work late and miss dinner with his family as a general policy. He made that one small decision every night, year after year. The decisions that we write off as momentary, insignificant, incidental, everyday encounters are exactly when we have a chance to define ourselves. To find beauty. To engage the world around us. To create memories.

Okay, so you're busy enough trying to make sure your kids are clean, fed, and properly dressed. You're fried. How can you possibly have time to bother with "creating memories" or whatever bullshit Teri Hatcher is prattling on about? It's all you can do to get through the day. You don't have time to think, much less creatively open your mind. But how much time are you spending, or will you spend, on regret? How much time goes to thinking *I should be doing this* or, later, *I should have done that*?

Getting older doesn't just change your body. It makes you reflect on your life. As I already mentioned, I didn't get to go to a place like Juilliard because my dad wanted me to be an electrical engineer. Needless to say, my all-time dream job was not to grow up and design electrical systems for wastewater treatment facilities. (Can you see me walking into a meeting and saying, "They're meeting underground injection control standards—and they're spectacular!") Though I did get off on getting higher test scores than the boys in my math classes. But it's not like I had a deep, irrefutable conviction that I *had* to be an actress, either. Truth be told, I actually never made the deliberate choice to be an actress. It wasn't my calling. It just sort of happened. But after that part as a mermaid on *The Love Boat* jumped into my lap, I worked hard at becoming a professional actress. Any job worth doing is worth doing well, after all. And being the A student that I am (okay, the B student, gimme a break), I try to do everything well. Still, I'll never forget that I didn't choose my career, at least not at first.

How did I wind up here? Well, where is "here"? For me it's being single at forty, working hard, not getting asked to dinner regularly, feeling somewhat insecure, trying to make the world a better place, and raising a daughter. I could have been so many things other than an actress. I could have been a nonworking actress (actually I was, not long ago). I could have been a teacher, a businesswoman, a great wife with more children. I could have lived in Montana or Napa or Texas or Pennsylvania. I could have lived in a Craftsman house instead of the modern/'60s thing I've got going now. But I didn't. I know what you're thinking. It's hard to believe that I'd want another life. It may seem silly now, but for all the years before *Desperate Housewives* you may have agreed that I needed another career. I don't think I'm alone in this. Lots of people end up down a road that they never stopped to choose and find themselves thinking about that Talking Heads song:

> *And you may find yourself living in a shotgun shack*
> *And you may find yourself in another part of the world*
> *And you may find yourself behind the wheel of a large automobile*
> *And you may find yourself in a beautiful house, with a beautiful*
> *Wife*
> *And you may ask yourself—well . . . how did I get here?*

You have no idea how you got where you are or how to change direction without hurting anyone or losing your beautiful house or your beautiful spouse. Life just happens and you improvise from wherever you find yourself. It can be fifteen years later and you find yourself asking, "Why am I an accountant when I wanted to be a pilot?"

You can get hung up in the world of coulds and shoulds. "I should have . . ." is the worst of all. Man, that one gets me. When I'm lying in bed I can find myself wide awake at midnight, thinking about how I should have handled an argument I had twenty years ago with my father when he asked me, "How much did that thought cost you?" He was referring to the cost of the therapy I'd been getting in my twenties. I was trying to learn to set some boundaries in the unhealthily fused relationship I had with my parents. Well, I blew up and told them to leave my house and never come back. Of course that's not what I wanted, I just wanted them to respect me and my space. I'm not saying I didn't act appropriately in that situation, but I do rethink those dramatic times. I relive their pain and then I imagine all the ways it could have gone. What if my parents had died in a car accident right after they left? What if in anger I'd slipped in the tub and cracked my head open and now that my parents were never coming back I'd bleed to death? What if my dad had said, "Wow, I'm glad you're working on yourself and communicating your needs to be happy." Well, that wasn't my dad, but I could lie there all night and imagine it was. Late at night I tell myself I *should have* been calmer. I *should have* forgiven him and realized that he loved me, and he was doing the best he could. But I didn't. I got angry because I felt like my adulthood was being invaded. My house was ground where I should be respected and he was making fun of me. I didn't like it. Though he tries his best, he does create problems and isn't exactly . . . oh shit, now it's 2 A.M. and I've been thinking about this for the last hour. I've got to go back to sleep. Now I'll never get enough sleep to look good on camera. Then again, how good do you have to look when Superman is sweeping you through the clouds saving you from the bad guy?

The bad guy. So much for sleep. Next thing I know I'm off remembering that mugging I told you about. I *should have* used the valet. But I didn't, so some bad guy came out of nowhere, stuck a gun in my face, and said, "Give me your purse or I'll kill you." Needless to say, Superman didn't show. So of course I gave him my purse and he ran. The cops arrived, and in the middle of my nervous, shaking attempt to describe him, they asked me for my autograph.

Now I'm so anxious that my ears are hot and red and I can't sleep but I can't make anything better either. Did I set the alarm? Let me check. Okay, it's on—I never neglect to turn it on, but I always have to double and triple check. And then, what would I do if someone broke in? What if there were a fire? Would I set the parrot free or carry his cage out of the house? Would I leave Emerson outside alone when I came back in for the dogs? What if there were an earthquake? Clearly I need a fallout shelter. What have I been thinking all this time, living here without a fallout shelter?

Ping-ponging among scenarios, my restless mind turns to a time when I gathered up old clothes of mine and Emerson's—purses, shoes, whatever—for a local women's and kids' shelter. I'm proud that I've taught my daughter that it is good to give away. Throughout the year if she gets repeats of gifts for birthdays or holidays, we set them aside and give them to kids in need at Christmas. Anyway, this time she came into my room to say, "Mom, I think all those kids need these more than me." She proudly presented me with a big basket of dolls. When she left the room I began to look through the basket. As I looked I realized that some of the dolls, about a third of them, were vintage, sort of expensive dolls. I remembered the effort and cost I put into getting them for her. Now she's only thinking about whether she likes something right now. But I'm thinking about what happens when she wants it *back*, and how hard it will be to find it again. So while she's ready to give them away, for me it's hard to let go. Cut to the first lesson in this story: When your child is ready to let go of something, not only should you let them let it go, but you should let it go too.

Yeah, well, that's not advice that I heeded this time. I proceeded to sort through the dolls, removing the ones that I thought were too special to give away. I put them in a separate bag, thinking maybe she'd wake up one day and be sorry she got rid of them and then, ta-da! I'd be the hero and have them waiting for her. (Or I'd take the dolls to a resale store and exchange them for something she actually did want.) I know, I know. I've already admitted to the mistake I was making, so please refrain from judgment.

Anyway, somewhere in the process of gathering up everything for the shelter, the special vintage doll bag got thrown in with it (as Emerson had originally intended). A few days later I went looking for it and couldn't find it. When I realized it was gone, I had a massive anxiety attack about not being able to undo the thing that had been done. Now I'd never be able to give back those couple of dolls I just knew in my intuitive-mother heart that she was going to want. And it just ate me up. I stewed about it for hours, I admit with embarrassment. That's huge with me. That feeling of not being able to undo something. I try to control everything, to get everything right. It's hard when it doesn't go as planned. Well, finally, I just said, *Okay, I can't do anything about it. My daughter wanted this anyway. Why am I doing this? What is it I'm not letting go of?* And then I realized it was Emerson's childhood. It was her being a little girl. Her wanting some toy and the maternal joy of making her happy by finding it for her. It wasn't the dolls, it was the whole emotion that went with them. When I realized that, I was actually and genuinely ready to let go. It took me a few hours but I did it. I feel okay about it now. It was what was meant to be. I know that compared to losing your whole house in a fire or a hurricane, this seems ridiculously small, but most people thankfully and luckily don't have those huge disasters to deal with. For most of us it is these little struggles, these little events that happen when we don't have complete control, that are our lessons in letting go.

Oh . . . and now it's 3 A.M. This is what I'm talking about. You can *should* yourself right into the grave. So don't do it. Stop right now. No, I mean *right now*. Don't fall in the trap of saying, "I should have stopped shoulding five minutes ago." Believe me, it's a slippery slope. Instead, look at your life right now and choose to make it the life you want to have. Even if you've made mistakes, divorced someone you should have stayed with, not done your job well, gained too much weight, been a stressed-out mother—just choose to forgive yourself right now and change something. Like how you feel about your nipples! (God, my editor is just going to kill me on this nipple thing.)

As you can see from my midnight dwelling, I can't claim to succeed at this. I don't always have the answer. But I know this is the right question: How will you look back on this moment from your deathbed? On my deathbed, am I really going to care whether I saved dolls my daughter didn't even want? No! What I want to be able to say is, "I worked, but I made time to relax. I took care of my body and spirit. And I didn't let emails or credit card bills steal any of that valuable time away from myself. I traveled, I learned, I was kind, and I gave back." I'm not just telling you this for your sake. After all, I'm the one who's going to have to listen to you complaining from that other hospital bed. I hope we lie there saying, "Remember the time when I did . . ." So that instead of regretting our lives we just revel in them as we drift peacefully off into the ether.

We spend so much time multitasking—eating on the go or standing up in the kitchen, talking on cell phones as we run our errands, cleaning the kitchen as we talk to our kids, practicing lines while we shower (Wait, what? Everyone doesn't do that?)—that it's important to pick moments where we slow things down. You can't always make time for everything. That's impossible. But you can make slowing some things down a way of life. Like the last few days, I've been, literally, pouring chocolate into ten butterfly-shaped lollipop molds at a time, putting them in the fridge, then writing this book while they harden. I've got to go to work, record a Clairol voice-over, film a public service announcement about child abuse, film *Desperate Housewives*, finish this book draft, and then stay up all night making the rest of the three hundred lollipops for Emerson's school. So yes, today is not a good day to slow down. But some friends on the *Desperate Housewives* set will hear about all the balls I'm juggling and they'll say, "It's got to stop!" They're right, it will, and I'm aware that I can't go at this pace forever and that I do extend myself too much. But it's me. I try to do a lot, be a lot for everyone, and, well, on my deathbed I'll say I tried to help people. And that's okay, right? I mean I did walk away from that sewage mess I told you about. That's right, I just left it there for five hours and took my daughter to be in her first horse show. I knew I could take care of it when I got home, which I did, and that was a fabulous deathbed choice.

I get in lots of trouble because I don't always answer the phone. Lots of trouble is an understatement. I'm pretty sure some people hate me for being so hard to track down. A would-be boyfriend once told me I was harder to reach than President Bush (though I doubt he was in a position to know for sure). Remember in the olden days when there were busy signals? Now there's call-waiting, cell phones, email, IMs, text-messaging, BlackBerries—there's an expectation of getting ahold of people. I don't let myself be available 24-7—otherwise I could spend my whole life on the phone.

We live in a microwave society. Hot food in seconds. Velcro shoes. Video on demand. Instant everything. What does this do to us? What does it do to our kids? We push them into situations where they can't wait or aren't expected to wait. We speed them through life, and what's the result? They have no sense of delayed gratification. If you grow up without delayed gratification, you'll never have the patience to succeed in life. Good things take long-term investment and perseverance. Like my career. It took twenty years, people, twenty years.

I was in Napa once, well more than once—I love Napa and wine. But this time I was maybe twenty-five; I didn't have much money; I had driven up with a friend in my air-conditionless manual Ford

Probe. One day, we went bike-riding up and down the Napa Trail, tasting wine all the way. As the sun was setting, we rode back toward the hotel, when I looked down and noticed that a frog was hopping along faster than I was cycling. That's when I knew I'd had too much to drink and got off to walk. Thanks, froggie. Anyway, on that trip we bought a bottle of cabernet that the guy told us would be best to drink in ten years. At twenty-five, that seemed like a lifetime. Actually, it still does. What the hell, we bought it. Can you imagine looking at that bottle year after year, rotating it slightly, shipping it from LA to New York and back to LA? Ten years later, my friend and I finally drank that wine. And guess what? It was the best wine I'd ever tasted. We were drinking big glasses of patience. Red, smooth, delayed gratification, the memory of which would last us more than another decade. My latest long-term wine investment is a bottle I bought on my fortieth birthday trip that's tucked away awaiting my fiftieth. If you practice delayed gratification with luxuries like wine, it makes it easier to wait for those rare New York City double rainbows to come along.

After I had Emerson, a nutritionist told me she wanted me to start taking hour-long walks every day. I said, "So I need to start exercising?" She said, "No, this isn't exercise. That will come later. This is walking without a goal. Giving yourself time to hear a bird, see a tree, and, most importantly, to finish a thought." That's a real mother problem. We don't realize how interrupted we are by our children, cell phones, and obligations. Imagine—to actually be important enough to just "be" for an hour, to just think for an hour, not even for the double purpose of burning calories.

I did those hour-long walks for a long time, and now I've brought what I learned there to exercise. Exercise (I mean working out) is its own kind of delayed gratification. Don't you feel like every time you work out there should be immediate payback? *I did twenty crunches, now where's my flat stomach?* But no, apparently it's a long-term investment, some of which you see and some of which is going on inside your arteries. Still, there are ways to relish your experience along the way. Hiking and running make me feel strong and work my heart. But mostly they're the best way to let my mind go, to hear my thoughts in a way I can't with all the noise of the day. I recommend doing it without headphones—though periodically I need a little '80s disco to get my ass up a hill—but with no music, you really get a chance to be with yourself, and that's rewarding. You may not see instant results on your body, but you'll feel them in your spirit. You'll appreciate them on your deathbed, which might actually be a bit further away thanks to that modicum of exercise.

That nutritionist's advice wasn't just about exercising for my spirit. It was about creating space for myself. She must have been psychic and known somehow that I was incapable of taking a bath without reviewing a voters' guide. If you're stressed about all you have to get done, it helps to focus on just one thing at a time. Take baby steps. Be right where you are, finish that, and then move on to the next challenge instead of thinking ahead and letting the enormity of to-dos overwhelm you.

For years I never gave a thought to what I wore when I worked out. I figured, it's just going to get sweaty and gross. Who cares? Then things changed. Nowadays, any time I leave the house, I risk being photographed by paparazzi. It's part of the job, but as I've said, it really affects how I live my life—at least in my naïveté I sometimes let it overwhelm me. Workout clothes are one of those tiny choices that have a bigger deathbed relevance than you might think. The other day I wanted to go for a run up the hill behind my house and I realized the paparazzi were out there. I changed out of my scruffy clothes into cute camouflage shorts and an orange tank top. Yes, I'd rather not look like crap in magazines on newsstands across the nation. So sue me. But what I discovered was that wearing my little outfit kind of enhanced my run. Not because the paparazzi were watching. No siree, I left them in the dust! But I felt good about myself. I felt like a cute runner-girl instead of a baggy, saggy, used-up schlub.

I'm generally resistant to that whole dress-for-everything mentality. I've been known to wear pajamas to drop off Emerson at school. I'm all for old flannel shirts, and I don't like the notion that clothes can define you. It shouldn't matter what you look like. But going on that run in my cute outfit helped me see that it does. Not because of what other people think—it's not about comparing yourself to other women—but because of what you think of *yourself*. You should care about your appearance because of how it makes you feel. When I wore baggy clothes to the gym, I was trying to hide.

If I'd felt confident, maybe I would have gone to the gym looking and feeling hot. The irony is that spending an hour working out in clothes that make me feel put together and sexy actually boosts my self-confidence. Dressing nicely and taking care of myself informs my personal level of happiness. Changing the outside helps me redefine myself. Who do I want to be? How do I see myself in the mirror? Am I happy with my life? Changing the outside changes the inside.

By the way, I would thank the paparazzi for unwittingly teaching me this, but wait until I tell you what happened with the photos of me in the camouflage shorts. That photo was picked up by British papers, who ran articles saying that I was too skinny, if not anorexic, and that I was running for fear of losing my figure and my job. Then all the U.S. papers picked up on it and (because I'm my own publicist) I got emails from all of them saying "We've heard you're too skinny and have health problems. Can you comment?" My lawyer sent back the standard response, saying there's nothing wrong with me and we'll sue if they say there is. But I also sent an email to one of them saying, essentially, "Jeez. I'm the same weight I've been for the last seven years. I'm in good health. Hello? That's why I was jogging up a hill!" You can't win. If you're jogging, you're too thin. If you're on the beach in your bikini, you're too fat. Dressing for the paparazzi clearly does me no good. Just another reason to believe in myself and not worry what others think.

If you slog to the gym looking and feeling frumpy, you're feeding yourself two conflicting messages: a) I'm trying to be healthy and strong and b) I'm not worth taking care of, I'm not worth the time. Now there's a recipe for insanity. So I say, do it now. Give yourself the reward to inspire yourself. Do it to applaud where you are right now. Be nice to yourself today, because you're hauling your ass to the gym today, and you deserve it—today. It all adds up at the end of your life.

This Deathbed Decision stuff also comes to play in parenting. When you spend time with your child, you have infinite opportunities to slow things down, to make small choices with big meanings, to create memories. I'm not saying every drive to school has to be a heart-to-heart. Sometimes you know there's a conversation you could have—about sharing, or reading, or the guy whose job it is to invent new street signs—and you'd rather drive in silence. But every so often, when you see an opportunity, try to find the energy to have a moment with your child.

Children see things on such a micro level that it opens your own eyes to the lessons around you. When Emerson was about three, we got on a city bus going down Ninth Avenue. Some senior citizens got on after we did, so I told Emerson we had to get up and move to the back of the bus. She asked me why we had to move, and as we rode home, we had a long talk about respecting your elders. I told her that she should try to make things easier for other people whenever she had a chance. That was New York—full of unexpected opportunities.

Now, you might not have the opportunity for that conversation in LA, or any other part of the country where most people use cars for transportation. Cars are dehumanizing and isolating. They make us into extensions of them—extensions of cold, metal machines. It takes extra effort to find the lessons there, rather than teaching our kids defensive driving and road rage or sticking a DVD in the backseat so they can watch *The Incredibles* while you listen to directions from your GPS. When we drive in LA and Emerson—older now—asks me for things, I've started to say, "If I were an octopus . . ." and we talk about what I'd be doing with each of my eight tentacles—handing her Goldfish crackers, adjusting the radio, lowering the windows, wiping her nose, driving the car, picking up the toy she just dropped . . . you get the idea. I sure didn't do it the first time it happened, but after a while I figured out a fun, jokey way to teach her that I'm human. I only have two hands. And when I'm driving I keep them at ten o'clock and two o'clock. In theory.

Sometimes instead of just going on a walk with Emerson, we'll make a scavenger hunt for ourselves. We make each other lists of things we should try to spot: a brown leaf, a bottle cap, a red mailbox, a butterfly, a dog with spots. Once Emerson made one for me and she put "red-haired girl" on the list. After an hour of strolling the neighborhood I said, "I give up. I've seen blondes, brunettes, and a gray-haired man, but Ariel the mermaid doesn't live nearby—I'm not going to see a redhead." Not thirty seconds later Emerson yelled, "A redhead with a cell phone!" (Cell phone was on her list.) Sure enough, she'd spotted a woman with bright red hair talking on the phone as she drove past. Thank God Emerson's not so competitive that she kept it to herself—if we'd waited for me to find it, it would have been a very long walk.

Our scavenger hunts are healthy—we're walking, we're reading, we're writing. And they remind Emerson to see and appreciate the world around her. We even dropped in unannounced on a friend in the neighborhood. Nobody drops in anymore! I think we should do it more often. There's no better way to make people feel connected and special. We're all just trying to get dinner on the table, and it's always nice to remind and be reminded that our friends care about us, that they spontaneously think about us, that seeing each other and having a glass of lemonade or tea together is far more pleasurable than talking on the phone while multitasking. It's another way to slow things down.

At my best, this is how I like to spend time with my friends and my child. Nobody can do it every day. But the days add up and run together and before you know it you have a cell phone permanently glued to your ear—or at least a big knot in your shoulder from trying to hold it there. You're the person who snaps at the person in customer service when the line is too long. The last good book you read was *The Thornbirds*. You're not the person you wanted to be. Make it an option for yourself to stop and think what the different answers to a question from your child could be. Just make it an option in the pattern of how you respond. It's a choice you always have.

You know how kids can have fun anywhere? Give 'em a big box and it's an insta-fort. Used clothes are a costume trove. A riverbed is a chance to be an otter family. Kids have an amazing capacity to find adventure. As a parent, you can learn from this, and you can also do everything in your power to preserve it. As I've said about a hundred times, Emerson and I often go camping up the Pacific coast in our Scooby-Doo van. We have it down to a science. Most of the time. But one time we got absolutely filthy walking on Moonstone Beach in Cambria. By the time we arrived at our campsite in San Simeon State Park, we had sand in our hair and under our nails and, as an unfortunate testament to our environment, tar on our feet. Showers were sounding pretty good.

We set up camp, then gathered our pj's and walked through the dark, chilly night to the showers. The easier your life is, the more it should be a requirement that you have the experience of walking from your campsite to the showers and putting a quarter in to get hot water. It keeps you grounded. But the element I didn't factor in to my image of roughing it was the part where there was no hot water for the showers. No matter how many quarters we shoved into the little machine, only cold water came out. And it was freezing outside, not to mention inside (it's not like my '78 van has a heating system). We were tired from the long drive and the day at the beach. But our van is so tiny, and we were so sandy that there was just no way we were going back in there without a shower.

Okay. So now I could fall apart crying, or I could start laughing. That's where the choice comes in. And that's where I chose to remember that I wasn't just there to feed and clothe my child. I was there to help her make memories. I was there to help her become the best person she could be. Sure, the situation wasn't ideal, but if I whined and suffered, that would do two things. Short-term, it would only make the experience worse. (It also wouldn't change the temperature of the shower.) Long-term, it would show Emerson to deal with unexpected pitfalls by whining and suffering. So when Emerson and I were faced with those ice-cold showers, I took a second to process our situation, then I turned to her and said, "Okay, this is going to be the most freezing shower in the whole world, and boy is it going to feel . . . cold!"

We jumped into the shower, laughing and screaming, and took the fastest, most shivery showers in the history of man. Then we grabbed towels and ran as fast as we could to the van, where we put on every article of clothing we had and cuddled and giggled and tried to figure out whose toes were icier. At the end, we were as proud as Antarctic explorers who made it through the winter. We were heroes. Robert F. Scott without the death in the tent. Shackleton without the open-boat voyage. We were both thinking "We did it!" But she was thinking we had a great time and I was privately congratulating myself on a few extra achievements: not losing my cool (far from it!), finding the warmth in our situation, and making it part of how Emerson approaches her life. Yay me!—and I mean it.

Don't get me wrong. I'm so not perfect. I'm just pulling out some moments I'm proud of, because I try to remember and learn from them. It isn't always easy. When I drive Emerson to school in traffic, I hate to be late. And it's not just because I want my daughter to benefit from every single minute of her education. The truth is that I'm competitive about timeliness because sometimes her dad gets her to school late. So, in my insecurity, getting her there on time proves that I'm a better parent than he is. Which is, of course, ridiculous and misguided. (Really, he's a great dad.) As the traffic gets worse and the clock ticks closer to that bell, the tension builds. Emerson can feel it. She'll say, "Mommy, what's wrong?" And I'm thinking, *Oh, crap. She can feel it. She doesn't know what I'm thinking but she knows that I'm stressed.* So do I let it go, telling myself if we're late, we're late, and that it doesn't make me the lesser parent? Do I reaffirm to myself that I don't always have to be perfect? Or do I dump it out on my innocent daughter, grumbling that we're going to be late, hitting the steering wheel with my fist, and cursing the traffic? In the latter case, she is now stressed along with me—not because she doesn't understand the whole insecure, inner battle my mind is waging, but because she sees me worried and thinks there is actually something legitimate to worry about. Well, I have to admit that, depending on the day, either personality might win out. Sometimes both make appearances in the same fifteen minutes. Sometimes that ugly perfectionist rears her vein-popping forehead. Other times the calmer, more mature side talks that stressed-out lady off the edge, and it all becomes okay in the car. And plus we usually get there on time anyway.

As a single mom I've had to learn to fight every normal girly "Eek! There's a bug!" situation in my life. Whether it's the bees in my backyard or the imaginary sharks in the pool (which aren't bugs but fall into the same "Eek!" category), I don't want Emerson to inherit my fears. So I try to see them as a choice. The worst of all these encounters has to be the time I found a live lizard in my bedroom. When I noticed him, lazily sunning himself on the windowsill, a million thoughts flashed through my brain. *Oh my God, there's a lizard! It's alive! It has a very long tail! If it makes it into my closet I'll never be able to wear a closed toe shoe or boot again! Whatever you do, don't scream in front of*

Emerson! And *How the hell did it get up three stories past three cats?
What if it's just one in a litter of dozens of lizard babies who have decided to make my house their home?* In Emerson's presence, this internal freak-out was filtered into a completely fake calm. I told her, "Oh,
look! A lizard. Isn't that cute? We don't want to kill it, do we?" *(Yes, I
do! Let's just slam the sucker with a frying pan!)* "Let's catch him and
set him free." So I tried madly to capture it in a shoe box. It slipped
away, slithering under the bed, where I tried to prod it out with a golf
club that Tiger Woods gave me at a charity event. (I haven't had much
time to use it at the golf range, so at least it was getting some use.)
Then the lizard darted toward the Tora Bora of my bedroom—the
shoe closet. No way was I letting it get into my shoes! With a surge of
bravery I caught it with the box, slid a magazine under, flipped it over,
and calmly carried it down the stairs thinking, *Please don't hop out!
Please don't hop out!* while my daughter was deciding whether it
should have a boy name or a girl name. Success! Another fear half-
conquered.

Not only do rational (and irrational) fears get in my way, but exhaustion can, too. Emerson has helped me set the table for dinner since
she was three. It's worth the risk of broken dishes to show her that
she's a member of a family, that in a family there are expectations of
what you do for each other, and that she's not exempt by merit of being the youngest member. I don't reward her with an allowance, and
she doesn't "do chores." Chores are burdens, tasks you really don't
want to do. And while I understand there are always things you don't
want to do, I like to teach my daughter that there are efforts necessary
to achieve the desired results. I mean, eating dinner doesn't happen
without a plate. So it isn't a chore to set the table, because that would
be akin to saying it was a chore to eat dinner. Or birthday cake for that
matter. It gets served on a plate too. Clothes don't just miraculously
end up on a hanger in your closet, and the dog dies if you don't feed it.
So I like to think of this kind of expectation as a reality lesson in living

a life. And guess what? Helping your family can be fun. It makes everyone feel good about themselves when they matter, when people need them, when their efforts count. Being needed equals being important, and being important builds self-esteem. This is true in all our relationships and we should offer it whenever we can. (I'm much better about it with Emerson than I am with men.)

So—being needed. Building self-esteem. Yeah, well. The best laid schemes o' mice an' men . . . I can be pretty good at messing it up. Here's what happened: Not long ago, Emerson wanted to help me make dinner. I was home from work, tired, and in a hurry. I knew I could do it faster myself, and this time I just wanted to get it done. So I sent her off to set the table. But five seconds later (it seemed) she was back in the kitchen begging to help cook. Oh, all right. I asked her to do the couscous. It's from a box, and she's done it before. She measures out the water. I turn on the stove to bring it to a boil. She pours the couscous in. I turn the water off. She puts the cover on. It sits. (There, now you know how to divide up couscous labor with an almost-eight-year-old.)

But this time, when Emerson went to dump the box of couscous in the pot, she must have been in la-la land, because only half the couscous went into the pot. The rest went, well, everywhere. Deep in the stove burners. All over the floor. In the dog's water dish. Sand-sized particles crunched under my bare feet when I walked. I was tired. It was the end of a fourteen-hour filming day that had started at 5 A.M., but I still wanted to be the mom who cooks dinner, so I was pushing it. Every grain-filled footstep sent my rage-meter soaring. I hadn't finished preparing dinner, and now I had a big clean-up job ahead of me. I blew up—smoke out the ears and everything. I said, "Great, Emerson. Now I've got this huge mess," and sent her out of the kitchen. She went and sat quietly at the dining table, feeling really bad about herself. After five minutes of cleaning it up, I'd cooled down. Why should she be made to feel bad about spilling couscous? It was the first time she'd spilled couscous in her entire life. Wasn't she allowed to make a mistake? Now I had to fix it.

I went into the dining room and said, "I'm so sorry. That was way out of line. Let me tell you something about yourself. I know that you could put couscous in a pan nineteen times without spilling, and the twentieth time it's going to spill. You are an amazing kid, who is kind and honest and smart. You're a really good helper in the kitchen. Things go wrong for everyone once in a while. I completely over-reacted. I made a big mistake. I acted like cleaning up that mess of couscous was more important than hurting your feelings. It's not."

When you lose it with your kids, you can't undo it. You wish you could, but you can't. In fact, I'm pretty sure this will be one of those "I should have's . . ." that keeps me awake in the future. But all you can do is make it into an opportunity to show how grown-ups deal with their mistakes. I told Emerson there were a bunch of things that we'd learned from this experience. One: Mommy isn't perfect. She makes mistakes too. Two: When Mommy makes mistakes, she apologizes. Three: Mommy's very good at cleaning up dried couscous. And four: Emerson is quite capable of making couscous too. Then we went into the kitchen to make a new batch, so she knew that she could do it for herself, and that even if she messed up again, it was okay. This is one of the biggest, hardest challenges for parents. When you fight with a boyfriend or a friend or a spouse, it's a fair battle. He (or she) can defend himself. But when your kid does something that upsets you, and you have to sort through what she did wrong and what you did wrong, you have to step back and evaluate yourself. And then you have to be willing to confess your imperfections. It's tough, but you don't want to pass your bad habits on to your child.

I'm ashamed to tell the couscous story. I mean, really ashamed. So ashamed that I'm tempted to whitewash it out of the book. (It's *my*

book. Why should I torture myself?) Yes, it's much easier for me to admit being sent home by a premature ejaculator than to admit to having a Bad Mommy moment. I really want to be a perfect mother. But I'm here to be honest, and the truth is that I blew up, and other people do too. Though we still struggle to be perfect moms, it really isn't the greatest message to send to kids that you need to be perfect. It's too much pressure. The better message is to show them how you're imperfect and how you handle it. Do you spend the next week suffering? Do you apologize? Do you get over it? Do you find a way to laugh at it? What you do when you make mistakes is much more important than trying to be perfect. It's an imperfect world. Your kid has to be ready to face it. Warning: Use sparingly. You can't make the lesson of imperfection an excuse for bad behavior. That's cheating.

The good thing about parenting is that you usually get a second chance. The other day Emerson dropped a vintage crystal glass full of milk on the kitchen floor, where it shattered into a zillion pieces. This time I wasn't so frazzled and reactive. My immediate concern was whether she was hurt (she wasn't). Then I told her it was okay, that we all break stuff every now and then. It reminds us to be careful. She was obviously remembering the last of her kitchen mistakes, and I knew she was wondering if I was mad. Which of course made me feel guilty. But I took the opportunity to really hold her, let her know that I was not there to judge or to attack her, and that it *was* okay to make a mistake. There's a fine balance. You want to teach your kids to be careful and responsible. You want them to learn that things have value, but you need to find the right balance between teaching those lessons and the more emotional lessons about self-confidence, self-worth, and moving past mistakes. None of us should ever stop attending to and weighing these moments. This time, I could see that she knew she was loved, contained, safe, and forgiven. And if I could feel that way about her, then she could forgive herself too. Another "yay, me!" moment, thank God.

Every day, every moment is filled with choices. Choices of how to spend your time alone. Choices of how to deal with your kids. Choices of how to respond to difficult situations or to your own mistakes. Choices to multitask or slow down. A friend of mine always tells me that you get out of life what you put into it. This is true with your kids. The energy and thought you put into their lives is rewarded by the people they become. It's true for you and all the aspects of your day— your work and love and happiness and fulfillment. A zillion feather-weight choices that add up to the heavy truth of your life. And how does it all add up? I guess we'll have to answer that when we're lying in those hospital beds summing up our lives. We'll have time then.

Will Work for Pie

Ambition is the drive to get further, to have a better future, to succeed. When you're young and just starting to figure out what you want to do with your life, ambition is a healthy impulse. It's what motivates you. But Lyndon Baines Johnson once called ambition an "uncomfortable companion." Isn't that perfect? Believe me, I've rolled over on him in bed and it hurts. Not LBJ—he's dead—I mean ambition. It makes you realize that built into ambition is the ever-present seed of discontent. What I mean is, to want more is to be unsatisfied with what you have. That dissatisfaction is kind of useful in your twenties when you're trying to figure out your life.

But then you get older. If things go well, getting older means getting closer to accomplishing your goals. You might have the family that you once could only imagine. You might have a better job than the one you had when you were twenty. You might own a house. You might have a nest egg, the promise of Social Security (maybe—it's hard to tell how much longer that'll be around), and expectations of eventual retirement. So you grow up, you start moving toward a version of the future you imagined for yourself. Shouldn't your ambition be changing in response to your success? Instead of putting unrelenting pressure on you, it's time for ambition to start chilling out, going for walks on the beach, maybe doing some yoga or buying a time-share in Hawaii. Ambition has been working very hard, and now it needs a well-deserved vacation.

Just because you're older doesn't mean ambition tips its hat and heads on its merry way. You still think about that bigger house, more money, a better job, a flat-screen TV. I was explaining to a legendary guest star we had on our show how I've been since we worked together last season. And I have to interject how unbelievably lucky I am to get to work with him and others like him . . . yep, I'm really lucky to have my job. So, I was telling him that I've been fairly stretched thin (not physically—like I said it's all natural, no stretching required). I'm working hard, and it's all good: the being a single mom, the lollipop making, *Desperate Housewives*, Clairol, this book, a movie, helping raise money for hurricane victims, showing up at many charity events, shooting magazine covers, planning birthday parties, putting up Halloween decorations . . . basically I'm fried. And he said that he sympathized with the feeling that you have to take it while you can get it. Even at his age and with all his success, he's still taking jobs wondering if he should have, and why he did. Well, that's ambition. And maybe also classic actor insecurity. It's definitely a common feeling to think whatever you're doing at the moment will be your last job. Well, actually I did go so long feeling like I'd worked my last job that, now that people are interested, it's hard to say no. It's hard to trust that if I go along at the pace that makes me comfortable, one job at a time, there will actually be another job after this one is over.

Apparently there was a rumor going around about me wanting to leave *Desperate Housewives* to do movies. It's not true. False rumors always abound, but they're usually connecting me to boyfriends I've never even met. In fact, let me please state for the record: a) There are no catfights; b) I never renegotiated my contract or asked for more money. I don't make anywhere near the reported $285,000 an episode, and never have. I have no idea if I make more or less money than anyone else and I don't care; c) I am not nor have I ever been anorexic. I've never lost or gained significant weight except when I was pregnant. I'm not skinnier than I was in high school; d) I haven't had a boyfriend since my divorce and have hardly dated at all; and e) I'm not leaving *Desperate Housewives* to do movies or anything else. Most of what you read is crap because all I really do is plain old real life day-to-day stuff, and that's too boring for everyone to keep talking about. Even a reporter at *People* magazine once emailed me saying, "Please do something besides go to garage sales."

I found rumor "e" fascinating because it implies that I see *Desperate Housewives* as a stepping-stone to a better job. I had to laugh because *Desperate Housewives* is my dream job. I could not have a better-suited role for me to play. I work with people I like and respect. I have a seven-minute commute. I have plenty of time to spend with my daughter. And it's as steady a job as Hollywood can offer. Why would I mess with any of that?

Nonetheless, I have to admit that it's hard to put the reins on my ambitions. Ralph Waldo Emerson (one of my favorites) said, "Worry does not empty tomorrow of its sorrows, it empties today of its strength." I should have that one tattooed on my ass, only then I couldn't read it, or it'd be backward and I'd worry about why I was so lousy at backward-reading. It's hard to know when enough is enough. Yes, I love my job. But remember how I don't want to have plastic surgery in order to work? Shouldn't I be making plans for what I'll do instead? How much money is enough to raise my daughter? If all goes well, I'm less than halfway through my life. How much savings do I need to feel secure for the rest of it?

Wait! Don't throw down this book in disgust. I know I'm a successful Hollywood actress. I know I have nothing to worry about. I have far more than I need. I'm at a place where I can say, "This is enough." But consider this: I've never felt like I can count on anybody else. If you're dirt poor and you have a partner you love and who loves you, you feel safe. There is safety in love and companionship. If you don't have that, if you feel like no one ever stays, then you can count on two things: yourself and money. And so I've come to connect money with safety. If I failed myself, it was my own fault—my own lack of work, effort, or skill. I could blame myself, a familiar childhood feeling. I felt money would protect me, that I would never have to need or trust anyone else, but that's not true. I do need people. Money works—to a point—but it's limited. You can have all the money in the world and never feel the same level of comfort that you find in another human being. Money is a less-than-adequate substitute for love, but it's better than nothing. I never thought I'd be forty and have no one to go to dinner with, nor someone who loves me and whom I trust, but here I am.

Sad, but true. I'm only human, and part of being human is worrying about losing your job and taking care of your kids. Being human is losing track of what is enough. It's fighting the urge to always want more. It's struggling against the force of society that tells us (as the rumor mill tried to tell me) that whatever we're doing isn't enough and might slip away at any moment. It's hard to bid ambition farewell when my security company is recommending I move to a safer (meaning more expensive) house and Barbara Walters tells me she thinks it's time to upgrade my beloved VW to a fancy new motor home!

Our friends and neighbors applaud ambition. They rarely tell us to slow down. Laziness is considered a far greater sin. And yet, laziness and ambition—taken to the extreme—are opposite sides of the same coin. If you're too ambitious, you spend all your time working and jockeying and competing and assessing your status and wanting more. If you're too lazy, you spend all your time procrastinating and watching TV (not that watching TV is bad—please, keep watching TV!), shying from responsibility and feeling like a failure. But in both cases, you lose track of what's important. You fail to balance wanting to excel with being happy with what you have. You fail to balance ambition and satisfaction.

Sunglasses rarely fit me. I have a very small face. Small bones, a small frame. I'm just small. When you meet me in person, you see it. It's not unusual and it's not unhealthy. But I have big eyes and a small face, so it's hard to find sunglasses that fit. (Don't worry, I'm going *somewhere* with this. I'm past forty. I get to take my time.) I've always heard that Merv Griffin has said that to be a big star you have to have a big face. Julia Roberts? Check. Jim Carrey? Check. Marlon Brando? Check. Okay, they're all incredible actors. I'm not about to say that face size got them there. But I don't have a big face and have actually always wondered if that's true. I suppose the success of the last year of my life might dispute that little theory but the sunglasses thing brings me to the 2005 Emmys. (I told you. I'm taking it slow. I'm close to the end of this book and I'm in no hurry.)

Ah, the Emmys. In twenty years of being in the acting world, sometimes making a living and sometimes not, I never really imagined I would be nominated for an Emmy. Sure, I fantasized about that acceptance speech. That fantasy comes as a bonus in the envelope from the printer with your first head-shots. Anyway, this year—my fortieth—was full of career surprises. I was on a show that turned into a phenomenon, on magazine covers galore, and the proud, dazed winner of both the Golden Globe and Screen Actors Guild awards for best actress in a TV comedy (the latter all the more meaningful because it was voted on by my peers). I found myself going into shooting the second season of *Desperate Housewives* as one of five women nominated for an Emmy. And not only that, for maybe the first time in my life I was considered the front-runner instead of the underdog. People had bet real money that I would win. That made me uncomfortable because people were rooting for me in a race that was completely beyond my control. I couldn't make the horse go faster or plan out an offensive strategy that would secure my position. I was just showing up and doing my job and waiting for the votes like everyone else. Better to be the long shot—when you're the front-runner the only newsworthy thing you can do is disappoint and, well, lose! And that's just what I did. I lost.

After learning my lesson with the Golden Globes, I worked hard to curb my anticipation of failure. I told myself that I deserved to win. Not more than anyone else, but as much. I let myself hope. It was scary, but it was a risk I wanted to take. When they announced the winner, I felt a mix of emotions. I was genuinely happy for the winner. I recognized the surprise and gratification on her face from what I'd felt at the Globes, and I was happy to see a friend and colleague get that same thrill. In the same moment, I was realizing that I'd lost for all the people who'd counted on me to win—the fans, the businesspeople, the gamblers. (I could not get over that people lost serious money on me through no fault of mine, especially since I'm no gambler myself.) I felt more than disappointed. I felt embarrassed. Like I couldn't look my supporters in the eye. Like I'd done a bad job. That made it a hard night.

My friend told me to hold my head high and be full of the love I've always had for the show, for my part, for the TV industry. So I concentrated on that, and after a few margaritas and some good jokes from friends, I pulled through. The next morning I woke feeling relaxed and relieved. Then I saw, on the table, a gift that my stylist had brought over the night before. It was a pair of new sunglasses. (See? I didn't forget where I was going.) These sunglasses just so happened to be rose-colored. It was another great opportunity to choose how I wanted to look at this experience and who I wanted to be. So I put on those fabulous rose-colored glasses and decided that this was meant to be.

Losing was the perfect opportunity to teach my daughter that things don't always go your way, even when the odds seem to be in your favor. You can survive and move on. You can be generous and gracious and grateful for what you have, and losing doesn't have to take anything away from you at all. Winning might augment a moment or time in your life, but losing doesn't take anything away. That's the lesson for us and for our kids. You can't be a winner or a loser without getting off your ass and doing something with your life. Doing nothing is being a loser. Never trying is being a loser. Putting yourself out there means you're learning and growing and changing, and you might someday win. Not necessarily in the eyes of others, but in your own eyes.

I sent flowers to the winner. I felt love for my job and the people I worked with. Just then a friend called and said to me, "I'm proud of you for not wanting to lose." I know it kind of sounds like I thought I deserved to win, but that's not what he meant. This came from a very successful businessperson whose whole family is equally successful and nice too—so nice. He told me that was what his mother used to say to him and his siblings when they lost out on big things like awards. It made me think. Yeah, I guess not wanting to lose means you care about effort, about working hard, about being your best, and maybe even about being *the* best, and what's wrong with that? I remember a super-successful sports star telling me that he never wanted to win— he wanted to beat everyone. And at first that sounds awful, but when you think about it, it's the opposite of awful. It's the opposite of arrogant. It says—I'm ready to be responsible and work hard to be good. I don't want to win just so I can say I won. I want to earn the right to be the best, and I'm willing to work my ass off to do it. That's a good person, a person who doesn't think they deserve everything, but feels that there is a direct relationship between the effort one puts in and the rewards one reaps. Of course, the field of acting is more subjective than those of business and sports, but I like the sentiment. I consider myself fortunate to have friends who remind me of that, even as they support my natural tendency to say, "No, I don't even care about winning. I don't even want to win." It's a good balance.

I thought about how success is having friends who love and support you through the bad times so you can genuinely celebrate the good times. Success is being able to look at yourself in the mirror each morning knowing you've lived honestly, tried your best, and gotten to a place where you can look back and see a life you actually wanted to have. I can't say I didn't struggle with my familiar old mixed-up backward self-defeating anticipation of failure—with feeling ashamed that I even wanted to win—but I got to work through it, to pick myself up, brush off my J. Mendel gown, and know inside that I was worthy and that it was okay to like myself.

And in case you were wondering, no, the rose-tinted sunglasses didn't fit me well. They were way too big for my face. Or so people told me. But from my vantage point, behind those pretty lenses, they were just perfect.

When I think back to *Lois & Clark*, and how ambitious I was ten years ago, I realize that age, experience, and motherhood have changed the way I view success. I'm right in the job I want to be in. In the best moments, I have a sense of relaxation and comfort, a confidence that when this job is over, I'll deal with finding whatever's next. That doesn't mean my brain stops churning with the fears and pressures and hopes that comprise ambition. I'm still not comfortable with myself. My self-acceptance is still a daily struggle. But in terms of a job, it's enough. I no longer feel like I need to go be a movie star. Now if I do a movie, it won't be out of a desperate need for approval. It will be for the pure art and growth and camaraderie of it.

I'm reading C. S. Lewis's Narnia series with my daughter. The third book, *The Horse and His Boy*, tells the adventures of a boy named Shasta who, along with a talking horse named Bree, is trying to find his way to Narnia. Along the way they meet up with a princess who happens to have a talking horse of her own. (Talking horses are much more common in and around Narnia than in the United States. The only one I can think of here is Mr. Ed.) The group is attacked by a lion who, yes, is Aslan—C. S. Lewis's Christ figure. In this event he's preparing them for the unique lessons they each need to learn. When Aslan attacks, Shasta's horse, Bree, flees. But Shasta heroically leaps off and stays to save the princess. After the traumatic leonine encounter, the two kids and two horses are convalescing at the home of a local hermit. When they're all healed and ready to set off to Narnia, Bree balks. The old war horse says he's not going to Narnia. He says, "Slavery is all I'm fit for. How can I ever show my face among the free Horses of Narnia?—I who left a mare and a girl and a boy to be eaten by lions while I galloped all I could to save my own wretched skin!" But the wise hermit guy says, "My good Horse, you've lost nothing but your self-conceit. . . . But as long as you know you're nobody very special, you'll be a very decent sort of a horse."

The first time I had a major success—*Lois & Clark*—I thought I was that special. I was like that war horse. I had all these tales about how unique and fantastic my experience had been. I believed the hype about how great I was in a role and transferred that into thinking that I was the only person who could've done it. I was the main reason it was successful—or at least the main reason Lois was.

But the next time success came along, especially since it came after a humbling bunch of years as a has-been, I had the same realization as the horse Bree: I'm just not that special. I understand that my life and my career will have ups and downs. I know that opportunities get given and taken away. And I finally understand that success isn't necessarily a reflection of my talent or ability. I don't cause everything. There are many other actresses who could have made Susan and *Desperate Housewives* successful. That doesn't take away from my confidence that I've brought my own, unique, Teri-fied (and I don't mean scared) spin to the role. I just realize that others could have done well with her, and I get how lucky (and maybe deserving, but mostly lucky) I am. For all the ways the cards could have fallen, this time they went my way. I'm a part of something bigger than me. Like the world—we are important in it, but we are not the center. (That's actually a big ball of molten lava. By some, I might be considered hot, but not that hot. I am definitely not that hot.)

I'm not the center. Thinking you're the center is something psychiatrists say you give up when you're around age seven. Until then, for better or worse, you pretty much think everything is of your doing—and I guess that's the way we learn. Everyone laughs when we take our first steps and fall down, and we think we did something great. Believing that helps us build self-esteem. But we also think we might be the cause of someone hurting us, even when we aren't. That's why some confusing patterns emerge when we're young. As an only child I was especially prone to thinking I was the center of everything, good and bad. It's almost a relief now, at forty, to know that I'm not the cause of everything. Because understanding that I'm not important enough to be the sole reason for the success of *Desperate Housewives* also means I understand I'm not the reason for the bad stuff that happens. Not everything that happens to us in the world is a reflection of our efforts. So let's cut ourselves some slack.

My rocky career path taught me the same lesson that the talking horse learned from the hermit. But *your* career path might look different. Maybe it's a straight line, never getting better, never getting worse, and you're frustrated at how static your life is. Maybe you've always moved upward. Or maybe you've found yourself on an unexpected downward spiral. You need to take a step back and decide what "enough" means for you. Set reasonable goals, and when you get there, acknowledge your arrival. Acknowledge satisfaction. Revel in it. Spend time there, in the rare state of satisfaction. Resist the urge to want a bigger house. A bigger car. Surround sound. Don't keep moving your goals beyond what you've just achieved. You've got the

Volvo—don't worry about the Mercedes. Go for the bronze once in a while. Find satisfaction, but don't let ambition eclipse your life. You've earned a retirement. Spend time with your family. Garden or travel. Find the balance. Don't be complacent, but don't let your ego dominate. Success doesn't guarantee happiness. Happiness is work. You have to work at managing your ambition to make room for happiness.

My ambition helped get me where I am now, and now that I'm here I'm trying to let it fade gently. I'm trying to be honest with myself about what's enough. I certainly don't want a Ferrari or tons of new clothes. That's not me. But I haven't reached "enough" yet, because I don't feel secure about Emerson's future—her college, her kids. I'd like to be able to give her more. And for myself, I'd like to be able to travel, to give money and time to people less fortunate. I want more so I have more to give. I've been in the forgotten fields of acting before, and I know full well that I have to plan what to do if this is my last job. Yeah, maybe I'll age well. Maybe when I'm fifty or sixty I'll still be finding roles. Maybe I'll still enjoy it. But I know that's rare. I'm pretty conservative, and I have to figure that *Desperate Housewives* is, commercially and financially, the last and biggest opportunity I'm going to have. If I'm a smart businessperson I'll make the most of it and in the process generate more opportunities so acting won't be my only option. So if I find myself on the kitchen floor again, it'll be because I chose to spend the day polishing it.

One great thing about my job is that suddenly I'm in a good position to help worthy causes. I'm happy to let charities auction off a dinner with me. I've worked with a range of charities—women's shelters, homeless shelters, medical care for underprivileged people. There are plenty of big charities raising money for heart disease, cancer, and AIDS that change the world for millions of people. But sometimes it's also nice to work with charities that function on a smaller scale. I hosted a fundraiser for Pageant of the Masters. As part of an arts festival in Laguna Beach, the Pageant is an evening of "living pictures." Real people dress in costume and pose in unbelievably faithful re-creations of works of art by people like Edward Hopper and Norman Rockwell, like the *tableaux vivants* made famous by surrealists in the '20s.

Emerson and I got to be in one of the paintings, "Outside the House of Paquin" by Jean Beraud, and we helped raise $300,000 for the local nonprofit arts society that puts on the show every year. It was very nineteenth century, romantic, old-fashioned. What I remember most was the stillness. I remember being nervous that we had to hold perfectly still for ninety seconds. Now I know that doesn't sound like a lot, but I didn't know if I could do it—sort of that same feeling I have when I'm using the garbage disposal and one hand turns it on and I wonder if some maniac destructive part of my brain will just independently from my will take my other hand and shove it down while the blades are churning. Or like when I'm driving a car, I can have this private inner monologue going as I pass over a bridge, *You know, I could just swerve this car right off the road. Nothing is stopping me. I could just turn the wheel really fast and I'd never be able to turn it right again, and then it would be over, I'd be dead, I wonder what that would be like.* Then I'm across the bridge and of course I didn't do it. Being in that painting was like that—knowing I could do something but wondering if I'd blow it anyway.

Well, we got up there, and I was pretty sure Emerson was frozen in position. She loved her costume and really wanted to do this and do it right. So I was in position and my pose happened to be looking out at the audience. The lights came up, the audience applauded, the narrator was talking about the artist and the painting, and I was thinking, *There is the audience. They're looking at me. I wonder if they can see my hands shaking. I wonder what this painting looks like. Okay breathe, Teri, breathe. Don't lock your knees, you might pass out. How many seconds has that been? Wow, I'm in a painting—I'm a part of a painting! I wonder what it would be like to be on a wall in a museum*

just watching the people stroll by looking at me, and them not knowing that I could look at them too. And then I realized something—that I was quiet, quiet and still for ninety seconds, but in just that ninety seconds, I got to hear myself, to be in myself, to imagine and be still. All that came up—the thoughts and worries and imaginings and distance from my life—was beautiful. I'll never forget it. It was a good lesson that I know I've already talked about: We need to find time to slow down and be quiet. It's good for your mind. And they think doing charity work is just about giving; look at all I got out of it. It was fulfilling, and I'm glad I'm not so blinded by ambition that I can't take the time for such projects.

Not long afterward, Hurricane Katrina hit. I was taping service campaigns with CNN and ET when one of the cameramen came up to me. He said that he'd come to film the Pageant of the Masters as part of an ET story, and it had changed his life. This forty-year-old guy stood in front of me and told me that the Pageant of the Masters had opened his imagination and gave him hope for the world and his life. Then we spoke about how he works with inner city kids, and I had the idea that we should try to get a hundred of them down for the next year's show. He said that one night like that, one chance to see something so completely out of your world, can change you and help you for the rest of your life. And I believe him and am committed to doing that. When I travel, when I meet people outside the radius of my normal daily life, it changes me. It broadens me as a person. Even if a kid grows up in hardship, a single event on a single night can open a magical world of imagination that stays with him and inspires him for the rest of his life.

As we outgrow ambition for our own success, we can aspire to fulfill the hopes and dreams of others. It's a limitless outlet toward which we should all redirect our overactive ambitions. That's how I've started trying to channel my ambition. It's not about getting richer or having more stuff. It's not about getting further and further. It's about finding ways to recognize and be thankful for your success. It's about passing that gratitude on to others.

As we get closer to retirement, we can also return to the alternate lives that passed us by. What if my father had paid for Juilliard? Or what if I hadn't gotten the part on *The Love Boat*? My friend Joanne, who lives right up the street from me, was having a birthday party for her daughter, Emerson's friend. There were going to be six or seven second-grade girls there, and I decided it would be fun to give them all pedicures. It's straight uphill to get there, but it's too close to drive, so Emerson and I walked. I carried the pedicure tub and cleanser salt and pedicure tools and an assortment of nail polish options, plus a bottle of champagne (for the grown-ups) up that steep hill and arrived sweaty and panting. Then I set about my business. For every girl I cleaned the tub, filled it with hot water, and gave her a complete pedicure. This went on throughout the party. For three or four hours I just sat in that chair, painting nails, until I'd finished every girl. When I was done, the birthday girl turned to me and said, "If you stop getting work as an actress you could open a manicure shop. You're really good at this." She said it so sincerely, having no perception of the level of success I'm now enjoying. Joanne said, "Yeah, Teri, why don't you?" She was teasing me, but I thought, *I could. I could be very happy doing that.*

I have other fantasies for what I could do with my life. Don't we all? But the one I keep coming back to is running a café. I've always wanted to set up a roadside café in the middle of Nowhere, Montana. It would be a simple place, with a screen porch door that swings open with a squeak and shuts with a double bang. There'd be big glass windows across the front that look across the road to a view of endless trees. I'd hang up that tag-sale still life that's above my fireplace, and there'd have to be a mantel for my extensive salt-and-pepper–shaker collection. Folk music would be playing, and the place would fill with passersby and locals who came for lunch and stayed for dinner. It would be warm and cozy and I'd spend all day making comfort food:

pie, mashed potatoes, meat loaf, organic salad from the veggie garden out back, and fried chicken. At last I'd have an excuse to wear the vintage aprons that I've been collecting forever. They'd constantly be covered with flour. And in the fantasy I'd never get tired of cooking every day because every pie would come out fabulous. But when I needed a change of scene, I'd twist my hair up into a knot and stick a straw through to hold it in place, and come out of the kitchen to chat with the customers, asking about their days. Twenty years ago I was an excellent waitress. I loved chatting with the customers. Of course, restaurants are a hard business. What is it—90 percent of new restaurants fail in the first year? Leave it to me to come up with a fantasy life where the days are long and the stakes are way too high. Maybe I should content myself with the image of a house on a lake, with horses you can ride up into the mountains. I could see people or go for days seeing nobody. Eagles would fly around the house in quiet blue skies with no smog. I could just think. Be slow. Be old and tired and happy and done.

Afterword
Happy Enchilada

A few nights ago I was making chicken ('cause you can't eat pasta every night) for myself and Emerson and listening to a mix CD that a friend made for me. A song came on that made me laugh. I put down my spatula and went over to the stereo to play it again. It was the folk singer John Prine playing a song called "That's the Way That the World Goes 'Round." The chorus goes like this:

> *That's the way that the world goes 'round*
> *You're up one day, the next you're down*
> *It's a half an inch of water and you think you're gonna drown*
> *That's the way that the world goes 'round*

It's a sweet song, and I love its message. Life has its cycles. Little problems look big, then everything's okay again, and the world keeps turning. That's the way the world goes 'round. But on the album *John Prine Live*, he interrupts his singing of this song to tell a little story (like musicians always do in concert). He tells the audience that he was singing at a club when a woman came up to the stage and asked him to sing the song about the "happy enchilada." As he tells it, he said, "Jeez, I've never written a song about any kind of enchilada, let alone a happy enchilada." But she insists, saying, "No—you wrote a song about a happy enchilada." So he says, "Well, how's it go?" And she says, " 'It's a happy enchilada and you think you're gonna drown . . .' " So he sings the chorus again:

That's the way that the world goes 'round
You're up one day, the next you're down
It's a happy enchilada *and you think you're gonna drown*
That's the way that the world goes 'round.

Misheard lyrics are endlessly funny. I always thought the Eric Clapton song "Cocaine" went "She's all right, she's all right, she's all right . . . she's okay." (For those goody-goodies like me, the last line of the real lyric isn't "she's okay." It's "cocaine.") But the reason I love this particular mistake so much is because of what it does to the meaning of the song. Prine is already saying that life is unpredictable, that we're overly influenced by small changes, and that we should just roll with it. But then this *happy enchilada* enters the picture! And suddenly the problem isn't even a problem at all, it's a funny, smiling Mexican-rolled tortilla. That misguided, half-deaf woman walked up to John Prine and (figuratively) handed him this happy enchilada. And that's what the world is like. It's full of the magic of human interaction. Just when you think you're gonna drown, a stranger walks up to you and, *abracadabra!* turns your inch of water to an enchilada. There's joy in what you've got, even if you can't see it by yourself.

That's why I wrote this book. I want us to be there for each other, by accident and on purpose. I studied math, not physics, but I remember that for every action there's an equal and opposite reaction. You toss a ball up in the air, it comes back to the ground. You swing an ax at a tree, it slices the trunk. If you keep it up, you'll eventually chop it down. You throw a rock through a window . . . you get in big trouble. That's the way I see us affecting each other in life. (Well, not the getting in trouble part.) The intensity of your passion in the world, whether you build houses or raise children or manufacture computer chips, and that action creates consequences. Those consequences have their own effects. So in everything we do, we're responsible, as a community—for our planet, for our society, and for each other.

Energy is conserved. Sometimes I find that concept a little unnerving. I have a fair amount of bottled-up emotions. It's hard for me to just up and release that emotion. That's a pretty big action—who knows what kind of reaction it might cause? It feels so scary to just let that stuff go—to let the fears and worries and doubts of a lifetime out into the world without any ghostbusters on duty to protect innocent bystanders. In the introduction to this book I talked about how your life doesn't change on a schedule. It changes when opportunities present themselves. In the meantime you always have to work—to endure the gray periods, to take risks, to create memories, to appreciate what you have. Getting older—having those milestone birthdays like (ow) forty—reminds us to chip away at our own walls. That's what this book is meant to show. That day-by-day chipping away that brings me closer to *always* being the happy, complete, self-assured, sensuous woman I *sometimes* am. Chipping is hard labor. It's tiring, and you break a lot of fingernails. But sometimes a big opportunity—an earthquake of an opportunity—comes along, and you have a chance to pull down a big chunk of that unnecessary fortress that comes between you and happiness.

Just before I started writing this book, Emerson and I took a trip to Africa. I thought it would be a great, exotic adventure, and it was. I was determined not to rush through the trip, even though we were moving around a lot. I told Emerson that her one job was to help Mommy not do too much. That we could go slow and that would be okay. I didn't really expect her to take care of me that way. But in saying it aloud I hoped to get through to my unconscious. One morning, we were out on safari, just the driver, the tracker, Emerson, and me. The early morning sun was strong and low. The blond grasses of the savanna stretched to the edges of my vision, framed by the mountains. I didn't feel like a foreigner or a trespasser in these ancient lands. But I was so insignificant, so humble, that I felt completely buffered and safe. It reminded me of the feeling I had driving from Los Angeles to New York—the same sense of revelation. But now, instinctively, I knew what to do with it. The land felt massive and primordial. It seemed to be the beginning of everything. I suddenly felt confident that it could absorb whatever I released without causing any damage. I didn't want to dump my baggage on friends or a therapist or into my tightly woven world back home. But no matter what I released in Africa, it would be relatively small and harmless, absorbed by the continent's timeless fortitude. My fears, my painful memories, my doubts, my darkness—Africa felt like it could take it. Africa felt like it wouldn't even notice. So in my own little meditative moment, where I could have been alone in the middle of that vastness, I took a big, deep, slow breath in, and then I exhaled. And when I exhaled I tried to let it all go. All the anger, pain, regret, and sadness. All of it.

When we came home from Africa I was different. For the first time in a long time I started sleeping so soundly, so peacefully, that I felt like a new person. John Henry Newman said, "Fear not that your life will come to an end, but that it shall never have a beginning." That trip was a beginning for me. Africa isn't magic, but for me it harnessed the failures and struggles and revelations that had been tumbling around in my head. I was calm and clear-headed. I felt brave, and I was ready to jump off the cliff of writing this book. I've been honest here, and I've made myself vulnerable in a way that I often try to avoid. My reason for taking this risk, for exposing myself, is the same reason we all should expose ourselves. Love and truth go hand in hand. This is my attempt to do my part in bringing us closer. There is intimacy between strangers. I've seen it in the small interactions we have in the grocery store. I heard it in the voice of the biker who watched me jump off the bluff into the water. I felt it when the double rainbow spread itself across the Manhattan skies. It's my hope that my struggles, small and vain though they may be, can help build that solidarity.

When you come back from vacation, you feel relaxed and happy, and you tell yourself that you should get away more often. But then you get sucked back into the routine of your life and you forget until the next time. Well, I told enough people about Africa that a few months later they were asking, "Are you still hanging on to that Africa feeling? Are you still sleeping at night?" It's true that Africa has faded a little. My mind is starting to remember its favorite 3 A.M. workout. But part of what I let go in Africa is gone forever. The release was so powerful that the memory of that feeling has become something I can use to ground myself. Sort of like a mantra. I think of Africa, a place which was, is, and will always be bigger and stronger than I am. There's comfort in that. I'm not free-floating and alone. Africa is big enough to contain me and all my emotional litter. And so I urge you to look for the place or book or being that can do the same for you. Do the daily work. Make the small changes. Follow your chosen path. And, when the time is right, you'll find your Africa. When you release the weight of your past, you'll see that it still teaches you without controlling you. You're unburdened. You can appreciate being exactly where you are as you move in the direction you want to go. You can see what is, and what can be. Is. Will be. And that's enough.

Acknowledgments

No one accomplishes anything alone. Most of us are lucky enough to have at least a few friends or family to rely on for love and support. But along the way to becoming who you are, even the smallest, seemingly obscure interactions can unexpectedly direct your day and mood positively or negatively. It is in that light that I would like to first thank the traffic security guy at the entrance to Gate 2 at Universal where I film *Desperate Housewives*. Every day when I drive onto the lot he greets me with a graceful, choreographed salute, waving me through the guard gate, his big smile kicking off my workday experience. I also want to thank Art's Deli, Pace, and Firefly—favorite restaurants in which I jotted down book thoughts on napkins. Their owners and staff have accepted and nourished me both pre- and post-*Desperate Housewives*. I thank all the fans, who have rooted for me over the years and share my passion for comedy and second chances, and all the anonymous folk who've crossed the paths of my life and influenced me either to keep going or to get stronger. We are the accumulation of all our life lessons—warm and fuzzy, nauseating and sour. Without them, I'd have nothing to say.

Which leads me to the folks at Hyperion. The publishers who thought I had something to say. We all need someone to believe in us even when we don't believe in ourselves. Bob Miller, Kelly Notaras, and Hilary Liftin did just that. They listened, they laughed, they cried, they *edited*. Hilary guided my novice skills and honed my creative instincts. She endlessly encouraged me to finish writing this in my bravest manner. It was one of the hardest things I've ever done. I couldn't have done it without her. It's unusual and new for me to feel good about my work (see book for details), but I am quite proud of the result. More importantly, I'm proud to now consider these wonderful people my friends and to know that there is a foundation built for us to work together again.

My goal in writing this book was, well, a) not to go insane, but b) to communicate an honest tale of my journey to self-acceptance and, with hope, to inspire and maybe even lend a few tools to women out there who realize they have more in common with me than they thought.

Recently, I celebrated my forty-first birthday. As one usually doesn't throw quite the enormous bash one does turning forty, I shared an intimate evening with my closest friends. The ones who weren't physically there were very present in my heart. And man, am I lucky. I have got to be the single luckiest woman in the world to have such an array of amazing, generous, smart, and unique women and men who love me and let me love them. They know who they are, and this is the section where I get to say a big wet sloppy thanks to J, J, J, J, and J (yes, there are five J names), not to mention P&S, S, D, P, C, M, T, H, C, L, B, L, T, another S, another L, a V, and an R. (I mentioned earlier I'd never actually *say* who anyone was.) Except for Colleen Ross, whom I want to thank by name for stepping up to explore the unknown. You delivered and then some. Thank you, Colleen, for your beautiful illustrations. The book wouldn't be the same without them.

...ON/S.A. #109
W CLINTON AVE
SNO, CA
00205527

8/06/11   06:10:55

E/VISA
xxxxxxxxxxxx9263
Invoice#   2714501
Auth#   259789

Pump#: 4
  5.883 G @ $ 3.899
UNLE/Self $ 22.94

Total $ 22.94

  See application
  about how to EARN
  REWARDS with a
  Chevron and Texaco
  Personal
  Credit Card!

THANK YOU
PLEASE COME AGAIN

LINTON AVE
CA
85527

06:18:55   /11

E/VISA
xxxxxxxxxxx9263
Invoice# 271501
Auth# 259789

Pump#: 4
5.883 G @ $ 3.899
UNLE/Self $ 22.94

Total $ 22.94

see application
about how to EARN
REWARDS with a
Chevron and Texaco
Personal
Credit Card*

THANK YOU
PLEASE COME AGAIN

And to the cast and crew of *DH*, thank you for your endless effort and great ability to laugh in the face of the daunting task of getting all the work done. I wrote a lot of this book between scenes on the set, and I can only hope that humorous set vibe was channeled through me right onto the page.

I also want to thank all the business people in my life, who have of course become friends, and who have continued to believe in me and to create opportunities through thick and thin. Steve Small, Lydia Wills, Larry Rogers, Alan Wertheimer, and Barry Tyerman.

Emerson, I was a tired mommy while I wrote this book. I'm so thankful that you are the coolest kid in the world and not only dealt with my exhaustion but were so genuinely proud that your mommy was writing a book. Thank you, my love. And Mom and Dad, know that I love you and always wish you the best. Thank you for loving us.